Granada

Text
FERNANDO OLMEDO

EDICIONES
Aldeasa

Granada

5   **Short history**

13   **The Alhambra**
Environs and entrances. Alcazaba. Nasrid palaces. The Partal and the towers. Palace of Charles V, the Secano gardens. The Generalife.

35   **The Albaicin**
Plaza Nueva. Carrera del Darro, Albaicin Bajo. Albaicin Alto. The Sacromonte.

47   **The Centre**
From Gran Vía to Puerta Real. Plaza Bib Rambla. The Zacatín, the Alcaicería and Calle Oficios. Royal Chapel. Cathedral. The Sacrarium and the area around the Cathedral.

61   **Towards San Jerónimo and the Cartuja**
From the Trinidad to San Jerónimo. Monastery of San Jerónimo. San Juan de Dios and the Triunfo. The Cartuja.

69   **Around the Realejo and the Genil**
The Realejo. The Antequeruela. Towards the avenue and ways of the Genil. Science Park and Huerta de San Vicente.

77   **Excursions around the province**
Sierra Nevada. The Alpujarras. The Costa Tropical. La Vega and El Poniente. Guadix and the Marquesado.

87   **Practical guide**
Leisure, practical information

94   **Index of places and monuments**

Short history

Its impressive location at the foot of the Sierra Nevada, its monumental richness with the aroma of an extraordinary Arab legacy and the calm rhythm of a welcoming, vital and approachable local populace have made Granada one of the most seductive and attractive cities in Andalusia and the entire peninsula. This is something that was already well known by travellers throughout history and in particular by the romantic artists, for whom the city of the Alhambra became a veritable sanctuary.

With close-on a quarter of a million inhabitants, Granada is the fourth largest city in Andalusia. Situated at 740 metres altitude between the foothills of Sierra Nevada and the fertile lands irrigated by the River Genil, it possesses a Mediterranean-type climate with contrasts due to its height and inland position. The average annual temperature is around 15°C, and the monthly averages range between nearly 26°C in August and 6.5°C in January, with summer maximums that may reach 39°C and minimums of -4°C in winter. The annual number of hours of sunlight are 2,850 and the rainfall around 450 mm, with the episodic presence of snow which, of course, is always guaranteed on the highest peaks a step away from the capital.

The Albaicin.

From Iliberris to Garnata

The uncertainty regarding the distant origins of Granada has led to legends such as that of the founding of the city by Noah himself. Whatever the case, archaeology has been entrusted to show that its earliest days date back to midway through the first millennium BC, when the Iberian settlement of Iliberris was formed on the hill of the Albaicin. During Roman domination, the town rose to the category of municipality and it was given walls, a forum, basilica, temples and other buildings, with a periphery scattered with rural villas. At the same time it was one of the early focuses for Christianity, where the first Hispanic Council was held at the beginning of the 4th century. The importance of Iliberris – also called Ilbira or Elvira – did not decrease with the Visigoths or the arrival of the Muslims, who took over the city in 713 thanks to the collaboration of its numerous Jewish population, concentrated in the district known by the Arabs as Garnata Al-Yahud. It later became the main centre of the province of Elvira, one of the districts that Al-Andalus, Muslim Spain, was divided into. In the 11th century the city established itself with the definitive name of Garnata on becoming the capital of the Taifa kingdom of the Berber Zirids, emerging from the

disintegration of the Caliphate of Cordoba, who raised the Alcazaba Cadima – Old – and promoted the growth of the town in the shadow of its walls. The relief of Granada later increased under the Moroccan Almoravides Empire, which turned it into the main stronghold of their domains in Al-Andalus.

The capital of the Nasrid kingdom

Granada began its most splendid era in the 13th century. In 1238 the Nasrid leader established the

The Alhambra with Sierra Nevada in the background.

capital here of the kingdom that he had forged over what are today the provinces of Almería, Granada and Málaga and part of the neighbouring regions, at a time in which the Christian advance seemed uncontainable. In 1236, Ferdinand III had taken Cordoba and would soon do the same with Jaén and Seville. However, al-Ahmar and his successors, by means of skilful manoeuvring, were still capable of sustaining the last bastion of Islam on the Peninsula for more than 250 years.

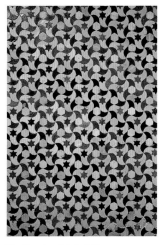

The Alhambra. Detail of tiling.

The Albaicin.

The Albaicin. Arco de las Pesas.

During this period Granada was a colourful, noisy and crowded city, one of the most highly populated in Western Europe, with thriving agriculture, a vigorous silo industry and intensive trade, a prosperity that was translated into unceasing urban growth. Alongside this, important artistic and cultural activity flourished. As a symbol of the Nasrid dynasty the imposing citadel of the Alhambra was erected, the precinct of powerful walls and palaces that overlooked the suburbs of the Albaicin from its height, the medinas, the old quarters of the Arab city, on the plain, the Jewish quarter and other districts that appeared close to the banks of the Genil.

Always subjected to the alternation between peaceful relationships and warlike conflicts with the Christians, the Nasrid kingdom reached the height of its influence in the 14th century and, in particular, under the governments of the sultans Yusuf I and Mohammed V, who achieved victories such as the taking of Algeciras and were responsible for the most brilliant constructions of the Alhambra. In the 15th century, however, the decline ensued. The continuous progress of the Castilians on the frontier and internal battles undermined their power in Granada, and in 1481 the Catholic Monarchs provoked the large-scale war to break out. On the 2nd of January 1492 the ill-fated sultan Boabdil handed over the keys of Granada to Isabella and Ferdinand. It was the closing act of nearly 800 years of Muslim presence on the Peninsula.

Plaza Bib Rambla.

Christian Granada

The resounding success of the taking of Granada attracted the attention of all Christianity, and for several decades the city was the focus of attention of the Spanish Crown. That same year, 1492, also bore witness to other memorable events, such as the contracts signed in the neighbouring town of Santa Fe between the Catholic Monarchs and Christopher Columbus that would lead to the discovery of America. Amid the tensions between conquerors and Muslims, which caused the uprising of the people of Granada in 1500, rapidly put down, the new authorities undertook a massive construction programme of monumental buildings with a highly symbolic content in order to turn Granada into a clearly Christian city: the Royal Chapel for the burial of Catholic Monarchs, the Cathedral, the Chancery, the Royal Hospital, the great monastery of San Jerónimo, as well as a great many other convents an churches, the majority of them consecrated over old mosques. These years of glory culminated in 1526 with the stay of Charles V in the Alhambra for his honeymoon and had its point of inflection in 1568 with the triggering off of the uprising of the moriscos, Muslims converted to Christianity. Their defeat and subsequent expulsion dealt a heavy blow to the capital and its old kingdom, the population and economy of which drastically reduced and undermined. The later development of Granada followed a routine rhythm of a regional capital dependant on agriculture and its role as an administrative centre, that is

The Alhambra. Plaque on Washington Irving's room.

until the sudden commotions and destruction caused by the War of Independence at the beginning of the 19th century.

Granada, romantic destination

The dawning of the Modern Era witnessed the romantic "discovery" of Granada. The magic of its Arab monuments, the dramatic naturalness of its emplacement, the picturesque traditionalism of its people and daily life, the gypsies and the soulfulness of their flamenco art captivated travellers and artists that painted it as a dreamlike place that just had to be visited, something that such popular works such as Tales of the Alhambra contributed to, written by Washington Irving, who portrayed an idealised city enwrapped by a halo of legend. The number of figures who answered this romantic and

orientalist call is uncountable, as is the growing number of tourists who came. Granada was at that time one of the main travellers' destinations in Spain and Europe, something that is still true today. Furthermore, in the second half of the 19th century and early 20th century, it benefited from the economic development deriving from the sugar industry and other agricultural and industrial activities, which was accompanied by a process of urban renewal. In the compact layout of the old quarter straight arterial lines were carved out forming the Gran Vía de Colón, while the enlargements and avenues channelled the city's expansion towards the outskirts. It was also a dynamic time in terms of cultural activity, with the presence of figures such as Ángel Ganivet, the multifaceted Federico García Lorca, the artist from Granada with the most uni-

Plaza Nueva. Royal Chancery.

versal projection, or the composer Manuel de Falla. This period came to an abrupt end with the mournful events of the Civil War, which included the death of Lorca. Just like other Andalusian capitals, the definitive modernisation of Granada occurred from the 1960s onwards, a process that speeded up at the turn of the century. Today the rich heritage of its historic centre, one of the most outstanding in Spain, and the vitality of its traditions, such as the spectacular Easter and Corpus Christi celebrations, is combined with the modernity of its infrastructures and services, fully maintaining the charm that has given the city its much-deserved fame.

The Alhambra

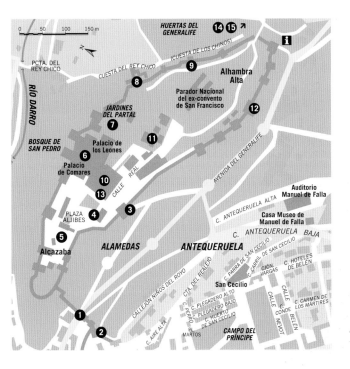

1. Gateway of the Pomegranates
2. Bermeja Towers
3. Justice Gateway
4. Wine Gateway
5. Parade Ground
6. Nasrid Palaces
7. The Partal
8. Picos Tower
9. Tower of the Captive
10. Palace of Charles V
11. Church of Santa María de la Alhambra
12. Gateway of the Seven Floors
13. Museum of the Alhambra and Fine Arts Museum
14. El Generalife
15. Water Stairway

Generalife. Courtyard of the Acequia.

On the Sabika hill, which rises between the courses of the rivers Darro and Genil overlooking Granada, stands the Alhambra, a sublime jewel declared a World Heritage Site in 1984 that features as the most-visited monument in Spain. It comprises an extensive fortified precinct measuring 700 m length by 200 m width, with a periphery of 2,200 metres of walls reinforced by almost thirty towers and magnificent palaces, gardens and other buildings. Along the steep surrounding slopes there is also an outer perimeter of walls and bastions: a massive complex considered the most remarkable testimony to Al-Andalus civilisation and a master work of Islamic art in the western world.

The complex is the result of a long history that goes back to when the Nasrid emir Ibn al-Ahmar established himself in Granada in 1238 and ordered a fortress to be built for his court on the hill next to that of the Albaicin over previously built constructions. From this nucleus, his successors enlarged the precinct until forming a courtly citadel possessing all the facilities befitting a medieval town, with walls, castle, palaces for the royal family and aristocracy, servant districts, mosques, baths, schools and exchange markets, as well as a network of streets, a channelled water supply, orchards and cemetery. After this early boost in the 13th century, the sultans Yusuf I

The Alhambra from Albaicin.

VISITING THE ALHAMBRA
There are several approaches that can be made in order to visit the Alhambra. The route by car goes on a ring road until reaching the car park alongside the Generalife, whereas the pedestrian accesses climb up the hills that cross the wood of the Alhambra from the Plaza Nueva or from the Realejo district. It is a good idea to book the visit and purchase the tickets in advance, by telephone, Internet or any branch of the BBVA bank.

Cuesta de los Chinos and Water Tower.

Gateway of the Pomegranates.

and Mohammed V, whose reigns between 1333 and 1391 signalled the age of splendour of the Nasrid kingdom, promoted the works that gave the Alhambra its almost definitive appearance, completed by minor interventions in the period of decline that continued until the Christian conquest. Later, the Catholic Monarchs and Charles V undertook some reforms and works on the Nasrid monument, mistreated after due to abandonment and by the French army during the War of Independence. On becoming the object of admiration by artists and travellers, its gradual recovery began, which has continued until the present. Despites its ups and downs, the Alhambra preserves the grandeur that it acquired during the Nasrid era, as can be appreciated by wandering around its different parts: the wood and the entrances, the Alcazaba, the Nasrid palaces, the Partal, the towers and the Secano gardens or Alhambra Alta, the Palace of Charles V, and the Generalife.

Environs and entrances

The most well-known entrance to the Alhambra climbs up from Plaza Nueva by the **Gomérez Hill,** where the typical Granada arts and crafts shops are in rows, like a bazaar, until reaching the **Gateway of the Pomegranates,** a Renaissance archway with the open pomegranates – a symbol of the city – designed by Pedro Machuca around 1536. It leads to the **wood** planted in the Christian era and, above all, as from the 19th century. To the south, the **Bermejas Towers** stand out, an 8th-century bastion rebuilt in the 13th century that protected the side of the Alhambra above the Jewish quarter of Mauror. The slopes, between irrigation chan-

Gateway of Justice.

Pillar of Charles V.

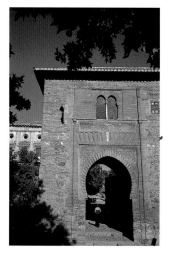

Gateway of Wine.

nels, cross the wood climbing until the **Pillar of Charles V,** the monumental fountain designed by Pedro Machuca and sculpted by Niccolo da Corte in 1543, with three figureheads of the rivers of Granada: the Darro, Genil and Beiro. Beside it is raised the enormous **Gateway of Justice,** the main entrance to the Alhambra built in 1348 by Yusuf I.

On the façade archway the engraving of a hand can be made out, an emblem of the precepts of Koranic law – a single God, prayer, charity, fasting and pilgrimage to Mecca – and an amulet against the evil eye, while in the next arch there is the key, the heraldic sign of the Nasrid dynasty, as well as being the symbol of wisdom and of the entrance to paradise. Above it was later placed an effigy of the Virgin to proclaim the Christian victory. Beneath the horseshoe arches is a passage with a bend that leads to the inside of the walled precinct, until the **Gateway of Wine,** on of the most graceful and earliest, from the 13th century, situated before the **Plaza de los Aljibes,** the esplanade with underground cisterns that separate the Alcazaba from the palatinate and urban area of the Alhambra.

Military district of the Alcazaba (Parade Ground).

Sentry Tower and Parade Ground.

Alcazaba

On the spur of the Alhambra hill is the Alcazaba, an early project and military stronghold, built by al-Ahmar, the first Nasrid king, in the mid-12th century over fortifications dating from the 9th-11th centuries, in turn built over Roman foundations.

On a triangular ground plan and double-walled precinct, it encloses a **Parade Ground** with the remains of a military district for the garrison and the dungeon for prisoners. The perimeter features a dozen towers, with emphasis on the Keep, the oldest, with fragments dating from the 9th century, the **Arms Tower,** facing the Albaicin, which protects the main entrance of the Alcazaba, and the **Sentry Tower,** the strongest and highest of them all at 27 metres which stands out at the fore of the fortress and was used as the residence of the fist sultans. Crowned

by the bell that controlled the irrigation shifts of the Vega, the terrace of this watchtower provides the best views over the city, the Vega, the mountain range and the selfsame Alhambra. It is a view that should not be missed. On one side of the Alcazaba grows the **garden of the Adarves,** planted in the 17th century in the moat that flanked the fortification.

AL-HAMRA, THE RED

The name of the Alambra, which it was given from the beginning of its construction in the 13th century, comes from the Arab *al-hamra,* "the red". This name seems to reflect the reddish aspect of its walls due to the shade of the materials used, although according to other interpretations the name is in fact the feminine version of the nickname by which its founder was known, the emir Ibn al-Ahmar, from *al-hamar,* "the ginger".

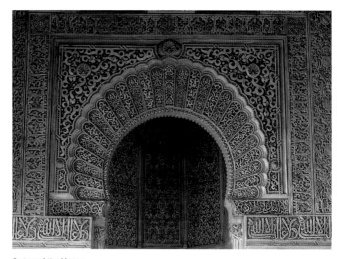

Oratory of the Mexuar.

Nasrid Palaces

The heart of the Alhambra is made up of royal palaces. Unlike the majority of European regal residences, the Nasrid Royal House does not possess large façades and a central axis that gives a hierarchical structure to its buildings; its ground plan rather responds to the random chain of circumstances that led to the construction according to the requirements of the time, without being attached to any preconceived project for the whole. Of the palaces that formed the complex, three have been preserved (Mexuar, Comares and Leones) as well as parts of others which, nevertheless, reflect all their grandeur. Each sector had a different function, from the public audiences and the courtly ceremonies through to the domestic use of the royal family.

A doorway alongside the **Machuca Courtyard,** thus named because this is where the architect of the Palace of Charles V lived, situated opposite, leads to that of **Mexuar,** the oldest sector of the Nasrid Royal House, with a 13th-century nucleus, greatly reformed and enlarged in the 14th century and in the Christian era. It comprises the **Mexuar Hall,** where the Royal Courts and Council were held, with plasterwork and wooden frames and morisco tiling from the 16th century, a small **oratory** full of plasterwork from the mid-14th century that leans out over the Albaicin, and the **Golden Room** with a magnificent ceiling and gallery that leads to the Mexuar courtyard. This is where the **Comares Façade** is positioned, a sparkling compendium of Nasrid art with ceramic tiling, plasterwork with arabesque and inscriptions – reciting the short prayer "Only Allah is victorious"– and marvellous carved wooden eaves. With

Mirador del Oratory of the Mexuar.

Mexuar Courtyard and façade of the Comares Palace.

Arrayanes Courtyard and Comares Tower.

an enigmatic positioning of the doorways, with references to a legend in Arab that says, "My position is that of the crown and my doorway a fork: the West thinks that the East is within me...", and was ordered to be placed by Mohammed V to commemorate the taking of Algeciras by Granada in 1369.

From this façade a passageway leads to the **Comares Palace,** the epicentre of the Alhambra created by the sultans Yusuf I and Mohammed V in the mid-14th century. It is arranged around the rectangular **Arrayanes Courtyard,** or the Alberca courtyard, an aquatic mirror between beds of myrtles where the image of the **Comares Tower** is reflected, the throne's base. An archway and the **Barca Room** – from the Arab *baraka,* the blessing –, with exquisite ornamentation of stuccos and tiling, mocarabe arches -prismatic

pieces modelled in plaster – and small windows with trellises precede the **Ambassadors Hall,** the main chamber of the large tower of the Alhambra, 45 metres high. With windows like niches on the sides and an unsurpassable decorative display in plaster and ceramic that includes poetic inscriptions, the room is covered

WASHINGTON IRVING

The writer and North American diplomat Washington Irving (1783-1859) personified the typical romantic traveller. Seduced by the spell of Muslim Spain, he spent a long time in Granada, living in the Emperor of the Alhambra's chambers. There he wrote his most famous work, *Tales of the Alhambra,* which did so much to spread the romantic image of Andalusia.

Arrayanes Courtyard.

Arrayanes Courtyard. Detail of tiling.

with a spectacular dome in polychrome cedar wood that represents the seven heavens of the Koran, with the white circle of Paradise in the centre.

The magic of the Alhambra reaches its zenith in the adjoining **Palace of the Lions,** the private home of the sultan that Mohammed V had built around

1377. Packed with the symbolism of the eastern civilisations, it shows the fantasy of the oasis of paradise by means of a fountain supported by lions, which gives the spot its name, surrounded by an imaginary palm grove of 124 marble columns and curtains of arches cast in plaster. On the sides advance two arbours and

Washington Irving Room.

THE ROYAL BATHS

Built in the mid-14th century by Yusuf I
as part of the Palace of Comares, it was
the place for social and diplomatic relationships as well as for purification and
relaxation. In line with the plan for this
type of establishment, although in this
case rather more elaborate, it is made
up of a room for undressing – the Camas
Room –, here with an upper gallery for
musicians, a cold room, warm room and
hot room, as well as the corresponding
rooms for the bath attendant, boilers
and stove for heating the water.
Outstanding is the refined plaster and
ceramic decoration beneath the vaults
with overhead skylights.

that conjures up the turning of the
stars with their play of light and
shade. To the east is the **King's
Hall,** divided into three spaces,
beneath vaults covered with rare
paintings on leather with scenes of
the Nasrid kings. To the north is
the Lions' Courtyard, the **Hall of
the Two Sisters** is adorned with a
spectacular dome; perhaps put
aside for the favourites, it leads to
the high rooms of the harem and
with the delicious view from the
Lindaraja Viewpoint – the "eyes of
the house of Aixa" –, a room covered with the most exquisite plasterwork with poems and tiling of
an exceptional delicateness. Right
alongside the Hall of the Two
Sisters are the **Emperor's Rooms,**
prepared for the stay of Charles V
in the Alhambra in 1526. There
are several rooms decorated with
alfresco paintings and Flemish coffered ceilings around the pleasant
Reja and Lindaraja courtyards.
Over the rampart hangs the
Queen's Dressing Room, a magnificent viewpoint over the Albaicin.
The tour of the palace's rooms
ends in the **Royal Baths.**

The Partal and the towers

Alongside the palaces that have
been fully preserved, there are
vestiges of others in a garden area
closed off by city walls and
towers. The first one is the **Partal,**
an Arab word that means
"gateway", in reference to that of
the Damas Tower, a pavilion
preceded by a gallery of columns

magnificent chambers are distrib-
uted around it. To the south is the
Abencerrajes Hall, which seems
to be the sultan's bed chamber,
where, as legend tells, 36 knights
of this clan had their throats slit
for the adultery that one of them
committed with the sultana.
Centred by a fountain, it is closed
off by a sparkling mocarabe dome

Lions' Courtyard.

Dome of the hall of the Two Sisters.

Towers of Cadí and the Picos.

before a rectangular pool. This is all that remains of a palace dating from the reign of Mohammed III (early 14th century), one of the earliest of the Alhambra. Spread around it are different constructions from the same century, such as a group of houses with signs of wall paintings and the oratory of the Partal, a small mosque on the

The Partal.

edge of the wall with extremely refined plasterwork. To the side of the Partal, between hedges and flower beds, blossom the remains of the **Palace of Yusuf III,** built at the beginning of the 15th century. This is where the Christian governors of the Alhambra lived, the Counts of Tendilla, which, after their downfall amid disgrace, were demolished before being abandoned in the 18th century. Going towards the Generalife, the circuit of stronghold walls continues by the **Picos Tower** and others that contain splendid small palaces. This is the **Tower of the Cautiva,** built around 1340, with rooms covered with magnificent stuccos and tiling. According to the legend, this was the home Isabel de Solís, the Christian favourite of the sultan Muley Abul Hassan, and the **Tower of the Infantas,** one of the last Nasrid works of the Alhambra, built as late as the 15th century.

The Partal.

Damas Tower and gardens of the Partal.

Palace of Charles V.

Palace of Charles V, the Secano

The scale, style and materials of the **Palace of Charles V** provide a marked contrast with the Nasrid palaces. Conceived during the Emperor's stay in 1526, the aim of this work, as exceptional as it is polemical, which, nevertheless, hardly affected the pre-existent buildings, was that of enlarging the Alhambra with an imperial house in line with the European taste of the time. The architect Pedro Machuca, trained in Italy, planned a majestic Renaissance building with a square ground plan with a circular courtyard and façades with dressed ashlar stone, windows and oculus. The building, started in 1527, progressed throughout the 16th century with the cooperation of other master builders, such as Juan de Orea, not being finally covered until the 20th century. Of note in the

> **MUSEUM OF FINE ARTS**
>
> The top floor of the Palace of Charles V houses paintings from the 15th to 20th centuries, above all representing the Granada school. It features the *Triptych of the Gran Capitán,* canvases by Sánchez Cotán such as the still-life of the thistle, paintings and sculptures by Alonso and other Baroque masters, as well as a collection from the 19th and 20th centuries with works that range from costumbrismo, traditional painting and landscape painting by Fortuny or Muñoz Degrain to the modernity of Manuel Ángeles Ortiz.

palace are the gateway before the Plaza de los Aljibes, with relief work glorifying the figure of Charles V and his victory over Francoise I of France, and the central circle of the courtyard with galleries superimposed of Doric and Ionic columns.

The **Calle Real** runs from the Gateway of Wine and the Palace

Courtyard of the Palace of Charles V.

of Charles V, formerly the main street of the area along which there are buildings of note such as the **church of Santa María de la Alhambra,** built in the 16th and 17th centuries on the site of the main mosque of the citadel, the **Baths of Polinario** and the **former convent of San Francisco,** now a Parador hotel, founded in 1495 over a 14th-century Nasrid palace of which fragments can still be seen; here lay the remains of the Catholic Monarchs until they were moved to the Royal Chapel. Further on is the part of the Alhambra Alta known as the Secano gardens, where the

Church of Santa María de la Alhambra.

Generalife. Courtyard of the Acequia.

network of servants houses and service constructions were placed. The **Gateway of the Seven Floors** opens up in the walls of this section, one of the main entrances of the walled perimeter, through which the sultan Boabdil abandoned the Alhambra after the fall of Granada.

The Generalife

On the Sol hill at the back of the Alhambra, crowned by the castle of Santa Elena or "Moor's Chair", are the terracing of the Generalife, the leisure estate to which the kings of Spain retired during the summer. The origins of this oasis of peace, the name of which comes from the Arab *djennat al-arif*, "garden of the architect", or as some would say, "garden of paradise", date back to the late-13th or early-14th century, when its construction was ordered under the reign of Ishmael I. The Nasrid

nucleus of the Generalife has been maintained, even though its orchards and gardens dwindled in extension and experienced important changes right up to the 20th century.

The romantic **Paseo de los Cipreses** (19th century) goes from the entrance along the **New or**

Paseo de los Cipreses.

New Gardens of the Generalife.

Central viewpoint of the Generalife.

Low Gardens, arranged in 1931 from Italian inspiration with cypresses, fruit trees, hedges, ponds and an amphitheatre for concerts and performances. On the upper terraces is the **Palace of the Generalife,** surrounded by more secluded gardens. The **Courtyard of Polo,** the pied-á-terre, and another smaller one make up the anteroom of the palace complex, ordered according to the Nasrid courtyard with a rectangular pond, vegetation and buildings at the ends. It is the **Courtyard of the Acequia,** one of the beautiful examples of Al-Andalus garden, recalling the Muslim ideal of the closed paradise. On one side is the pavilion where it is thought the harem and guests' rooms were placed, and on the other side, the **north pavilion,** with the sovereigns' rooms. It comprises an arcade of plaster arches over columns, a doorway with an inscription referring to its construction by Ishmael I around 1319, the Royal Hall and a viewpoint over the Alhambra, the Darro and the Albaicin. Alongside this pavilion is the **Courtyard of the Sultana** or Cypress, where the legend tells how the sultan's favourite had an affair with a knight from the Abencerraje clan, who on being discovered, caused the massacre of the members of his family. Above the palace climb the **High Gardens** scored by the **Water Stairway,** the flight of steps below a canopy of laurels, the handrails of which are channels along which runs the water.

Courtyard of the Sultana.

Water Stairway.

North Pavilion of the Generalife Palace.

The Albaicin

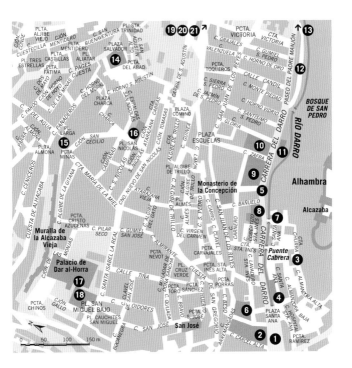

1. Plaza Nueva
2. Royal Chancery
3. District of the Almanzora
4. Church of Santa Ana y San Gil
5. Carrera del Darro
6. Casa de los Pisa
7. Cadí Bridge
8. El Bañuelo
9. Convent of Santa Catalina de Zafra
10. Casa de Castril (Archaeological Museum)
11. Church of San Pedro y San Pablo
12. Paseo de los Tristes
13. Palace of the Córdoba
14. Church of the Salvador
15. Arco de las Pesas
16. Mirador de San Nicolás
17. Monastery of Santa Isabel la Real
18. Church of San Miguel Bajo
19. The Sacromonte
20. Hermitage of Santo Sepulcro
21. Abbey of the Sacromonte

The Albaicin.

Plaza Nueva.

ALBAICIN

There are two versions regarding the name of the oldest district in Granada. One says that it comes from the falconers' suburb *(al-Bayyazin in Arab)* which occupied part of the area; another theory states that it comes from the patronymic of the inhabitants of Baeza who were settled there alter the conquest of their city by the Castilians in the 13th century.

If the Alhambra represents the monumental nature of Islamic Granada, the district of Albaicin, sitting over the opposite hill, on the other side of the divide marked by the River Darro, conserves the urban essence of the Al-Andalus city like no other place, a reason why it was declared a World Heritage Site in 1994. The Plaza Nueva and the Carrera del Darro shape the lower part of the district, which rises forming a maze of hills and lanes, with the Sacromonte hill behind it.

Plaza Nueva

This square, always full of life, is the focal point between the Alhambra, the Albaicin, Carrera del Darro, Calle Elvira and the low part of the city, one of the main public spaces in the capital. It is embellished by the **Royal**

Plaza Nueva. The Chancery.

Church of Santa Ana y San Gil.

Chancery, the high court established in 1505 by the Catholic Monarchs, a balanced building of a classical style, which was built throughout the 16th century. Involved in the work were Diego de Siloe, to whom the harmonious Renaissance courtyard is attributed, and Francisco del Castillo, who designed the façade in 1587. Today it is the headquarters of the High Courts of Andalusia. Beside the arch through which the Darro passes underground are the narrow streets of the **district of the Almanzora,** with its endless number of bars and tea rooms, and the **church of Santa Ana y San Gil,** one of the parish churches established in 1501 and built by Diego de Siloe in 1537 over the site of a mosque. With its slender brick and tile tower, its magnificent Mudejar framework and its Plateresque doorway in stone, it is an excellent example of the mixing of styles, so common in the city.

Carrera del Darro, the Albaicin Bajo

The **Carrera del Darro,** which winds alongside the river parking the border of the **Albaicin Bajo,** is one of the most charming and picturesque ways in Granada, scattered, moreover, with interesting little corners from the very beginning. In a narrow street of the same name is the **Casa de los Pisa** (16th century), where

Mosque.

CASAS NAZARÍES AND MORISCAS

Nasrid and Moorish houses. In the narrow streets that drop from the Albaicin to Carrera del Darro there are several Nasrid or Moorish houses preserved, some of them fitted out as hotels, such as the houses in Calle Horno del Oro and Cuesta de la Victoria.

They often possess entrance halls and small central courtyards, sometimes with pools, flanked by arcades over columns and lintelled galleries.

Saint John of God died in 1550, turned into a museum with personal items belonging to the saint and exotic pieces that illustrate the missionary work of his religious order. Carrera del Darro later passes several small bridges and stately houses as far as the remains of the port of Los Tableros, or **Cadí Bridge** (11th century), which was connected to the walls of the Alhambra. Behind a modest façade beside it is hidden one of

ARCHAEOLOGICAL MUSEUM

Housed in the Casa de Castril, it possesses valuable items dating from prehistory to the Nasrid period, among which feature Bronze and Iron Age weapons and tools, Egyptian alabaster vases, Roman sculptures and a varied series of Islamic ceramics, along with an astrolabe from 1481, demonstrating the scientific level of Hispano-Islamic culture.

the oldest Arab baths on the peninsula, **the Bañuelo** or Walnut bath, ordered to be built in the 11th century by Samuel ibn Nagrela, the Jewish vizier of King Badis. It is a pure delight to wander around its rooms with arches over Roman, Visigoth and Arab capitals and with vaults beneath the faint light of the starred skylights. Two blocks on the **Convent of Santa Catalina de Zafra** (16th century) show us a church with a Renaissance doorway and includes amongst its chambers a 14th century Nasrid house with pool and galleries. This is in contrast to the **Casa de Castril** which one comes to next, a perfect example of the small palaces built by the Castilians during the 16th century, with a façade in relief work with Plateresque images. Dated 1539, it belonged to the Hernando de Zafra family, secretary of the Catholic Monarchs, and today home to the **Archaeological**

The Bañuelo. Arab baths.

Casa de Castril. Archaeological Museum.

Paseo de los Tristes.

Museum. The phrase "WAITING FOR HER IN HEAVEN", which can be read on a balcony, refers to the legend of the page boy who, after being discovered in a romance with the master's daughter, pleaded for clemency, being told in reply that he could wait for her in heaven after being hung from the balcony.

Church of S. Pedro y S. Pablo, and the Alhambra.

The beautiful **church of San Pedro y San Pablo,** the work of Juan de Maeda in 1567, with classicist doorway and extraordinary Mudejar coffered ceilings, and the convent of San Bernardo (16th century) narrow the Carrera del Darro before opening out in the **Paseo de los Tristes** (Passage of the Sad), where the funerals were held. This name contradicts the relaxing beauty of this extension with terraces that offer views of the Alhambra.

The Albaicin Alto

From the banks of the Darro, the **Cuesta del Chapiz** rises towards the Albaicin Alto. It is one of the widest side streets, although to delve into its network of streets, stairways and alleys you can take a thousand different paths that will always provide new views of the interior of the district and of the Alhambra, which appears closer with each step taken. At the beginning of the hill is the reconstruction of the **Cordoba Palace** and a little further up, on the corner, the **Casas del Chapiz,** Moorish homes dating from the 16th century with a courtyard and pool, arcade and wooden galleries that is home to the School of Arab Studies.

Leaving behind the alleyways and flights of steps that give us a glimpse of the mark of Islamic urban planning, the **church of the Salvador** is reached, the collegiate that in 1549 replaced the main mosque of the Albaicin, of which the washing courtyard is preserved (13th-15th centuries) with galleries of horseshoe arches attached to the Christian temple. The area close to the church of the Salvador is by now the heart of the Albaicin Alto, which has its most frequented and popular spot, at the end of the bustling

Cuesta del Chapiz.

Calle de Panaderos, in the **Plaza Larga,** the pole of attraction for bars, terraces and street markets, from which lead the Calle del Agua, one of the most typical, with the Casa de los Mascarones, and the **Cuesta de la Alhacaba,** flanked by the Zirid walls that end in the Doorway of Monaita

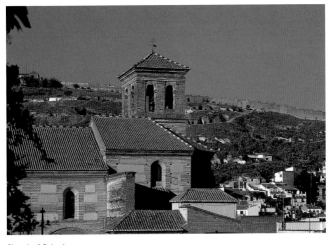

Church of Salvador.

Viewpoint of San Nicolás.

(11th century), a vestige of the Alcazaba Cadima or Old Castle, which protected the early site of the city. Just around a corner that also leads from the Plaza Larga one passes through the **Arch de las Pesas** (11th century), another gateway of the Alcazaba Vieja, and, by taking the **San Cecilio alleyway** or the Placeta de las Minas, you end up in the Plaza and **viewpoint of San Nicolás,** the privileged balcony from where one can appreciate one the best panoramic views of the Alhambra. Beside it stands the church of San Nicolás, another parish church built during the 16th century, of a Gothic-Mudejar style and, a little further back, the new

---

PALACE OF DAR AL-HORRA

In the quiet Callejón de las Monjas, at the back of the convent of Santa Isabel la Real, still standing is the Casa de la Sultana, or of the Señora, where Fatimah, the wife of Muley Abul Hassan and mother of Boabdil, the last King of Granada, lived. Built in the 15th century, it is constructed around a rectangular courtyard with a pond and arcades of arches over slender columns.

THE CARMEN

The word carmen comes from the Arab *karm,* which means orchard or vineyard, which finds its Nasrid origin as orchards with a construction to spend a period of time in. As time passed, the buildings were established as exquisite estates or villas with houses, extensive gardens on terraces, pavilions, forts and vantage points, until becoming one of the delights and symbols of Granada, abundant above all in the Albaicin.

Terraces in the Plaza de San Nicolás.

mosque of the Albaicin, which merges in with the houses of the district. The Camino Nuevo de San Nicolás, where in a small car-men, or villa, is the Max Moreau Museum, leads to the **monastery of Santa Isabel la Real,** founded in 1501 with a temple of a Gothic-style doorway and admirable Mudejar coffered ceilings. The adjoining space houses the **church of San Miguel Bajo,** built in 1528 to replace a mosque, facing the square that is one of the favourite meeting points in the district, with the Moorish Casa del Corralón on one of its corners. From here, it is well worth taking a look from the **viewpoint of La Lona,** which over-looks Granada, or to return along

Calle Calderería Nueva.

Church of San Miguel Bajo.

the sinuous maze of the Albaicin, by **Calle San José,** passing by the church, which uses as its bell tower the minaret (11th century) of the disappeared mosque of the Morabitos, until swooping and swerving down flights of steps, like an Arab souk in **Calles Caldererería Nueva** and **Vieja,** which are above **Calle Elvira,** the border with the low city, to connect up with Plaza Nueva.

The Sacromonte

Half way up Cuesta del Chapiz begins the Sacromonte path, running along the side of the hill going from the Darro. The first few bends reveal the surprising sight of its **cave district** excavated from the land, with the whitewashed façades adorned with flowerpots. Gypsies have lived here since the 18th century and later the caves of the Sacromonte were made famous by the gypsy dances and flamenco festivals to which all visitors to Granada should attend to experience the *duende,* the soul of flamenco song and dance. This unique setting preserves its form as it nears the Puente Quebrada ravine, and one can visit the cave of María la Canastera, open as a museum. Further on is the **hermitage of Santo Sepulcro** (17th century), the end of the Way of the Cross that marks out the path, and, trekking over slopes and turns, the **abbey of the Sacromonte** and **collegiate of de San Cecilio,** built from 1600 to commemorate the discovery of the enigmatic "lead books" that refer to the first Christian martyrs of Granada. It was later discovered to be a big fraud, but the extensive Baroque complex remained with church and cloisters where valuable manuscripts and works of art are kept, alongside the mysterious catacombs of the Holy Caves.

The Sacromonte.

Paths and house caves of the Sacromonte.

The Centre

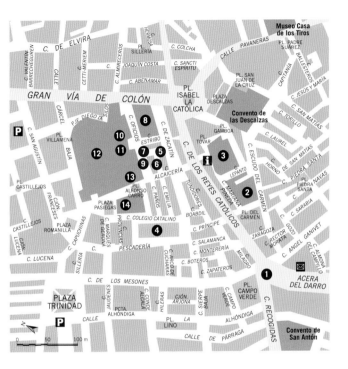

1. Puerta Real
2. City Hall
3. Corral del Carbón
4. Plaza Bib Rambla
5. El Zacatín
6. La Alcaicería
7. Calle Oficios
8. Madraza
9. Centro José Guerrero
10. Royal Chapel
11. Merchants' Exchange
12. Cathedral
13. Church of Sagrario
14. Ecclesiastical Curia

The Alcaicería.

The historic centre of Granada, heir to the medieval Arab town which was the focus, as it is today, of commerce and public activities, stretches out along the plane before the Albaicin and Alhambra hills. In its old and busy city centre, marked out by avenues and squares from the 19th and 20th centuries stand out the most important Christian monuments of the city, the Royal Chapel and the Cathedral, accompanied by buildings as representative as the Town Hall, and remnants of the Nasrid past such as the Corral del Carbón or the Madraza.

From Gran Vía to Puerta Real

The straight **Gran Vía de Colón,** the longest artery in the old quarter, full of shops and modernist buildings, leads to the **Plaza de Isabel la Católica,** where there is a monument by the sculptor Mariano Benlliure, from 1892, erected to commemorate the support that the Queen gave to Christopher Columbus during his stay in Granada and the signing of the Capitulations of Santa Fe in 1492, the agreement that made the first journey to America a possibility. Also meeting at this crossroads is **Calle Reyes Católicos,** the street that alternates between traditional and modern shops in its descent towards **Puerta Real,** the nerve centre from where the main streets and extensions

ÁNGEL GANIVET

A modern shopping street alongside the Puerta Real is Calle Ángel Ganivet, named in memory of the Granada writer who advocated the preservation of the essence of his birthplace – the subject matter of his most well-known work, Granada la Bella – and put forward the ideas for regeneration of the Generation of 98 group, and kept up a close relationship with Miguel de Unamuno. Born in 1865, he followed the diplomatic career and was consul in several places until taking his own life in Riga in 1898.

spread in all directions, towards the interior of the centre, the Genil, the Realejo and the outskirts. The name of Puerta Real recalls the presence in the place of the gateway, no longer there, through which Felipe IV entered the city in 1624.

Gran Vía de Colón.

Puerta Real.

On one side of Calle Reyes Católicos the **Plaza del Carmen** opens out, overlooked by the neo-classical façade of the **Town Hall,** the old 17th-century convent, of which the courtyard of column is preserved, transformed into a town hall in

Corral del Carbón.

1858. This square is the setting for public events such as the Festival of the Toma (Taking), which on the 2nd of January recalls the Christian conquest of Granada. Close by is a sector full of bars and interesting buildings, such as the Abrantes Palace (16th century) and, in Calle Mariana Pineda, the **Corral del Carbón,** the old Alhóndiga Gidida or New Corn Exchange, a unique example in Spain of the Muslim *funduq* or inn where merchants were put up with their products, and which was later a hostel for coal merchants, theatre and community centre, and at present, the head offices for cultural associations. This splendid 15th-century Hispano-Arab work has a large horseshoe arch with plasterwork at the front and a square courtyard with galleries over pillars.

Calle Oficios, alongside the cathedral.

Plaza Bib Rambla

Between Calle Reyes Católicos and the Cathedral is the most traditional stronghold in the centre, a complex grid of alleyways and main streets, such as Calle Mesones and the parallel Calle Alhóndiga where there are rows and rows of shops which pour out into the **Plaza Bib Rambla,** the most spacious in the old quarter, a recommendable pedestrian zone with the fountain of Neptune or of the Giants, the colourful flower stands and the coming and going of the cafés, restaurants and terraces that border it. The square took shape on the area of level ground next to the Puerta de la Rambla or del Arenal – in Arab *Bib Ramla* –, from the 16th century becoming the civil forum for celebrations, auto-da-fé, bullfighting and other festivals. It is one of the most important and pleasant spots of Granada.

The Zacatín, the Alcaicería and Calle Oficios

Adjacent to the Plaza Bib Rambla is the most traditional shopping area in Granada, the small streets in which the craftsmen's guilds and merchants thronged together in the Nasrid period, just like the souks of so many Muslim cities. The Calle del **Zacatín** – or of the second-hand-clothes dealers – is the nerve centre of this trading area that links up, via an arch with even narrower streets, with Calle de la **Alcaicería,** the area of Nasrid origin reserved for the luxury goods – silks, fabrics, gems – which after being destroyed by a fire in 1843 was partially rebuilt. Its picturesque shops, with slender columns and delicate stucco work, sell a diverse array of arts and crafts and typical souvenirs, from traditional ceramics and

Plaza de Bib Rambla.

Shops in the Alcaicería.

Exterior doorway of the Royal Chapel.

part one can make out the Old Town Hall or the **Madraza,** which went from being a Koranic school – *madraza* – founded in 1349 by Yusuf I to a Chapter House, between 1500 and the 19th century, which explains its diversity of styles. It therefore includes an Islamic oratory with plaster decoration, a chapter room from the 16th century beneath a Mudejar and Plateresque roof, while the façade and courtyard are 18th-century Baroque. Opposite the Madraza are the Royal Chapel and the Lonja, the exchange market.

marquetry objects to clothes, complements or miniature replicas of monuments.

Along the Alcaicería, and from the Plaza Bib Rambla or the Gran Vía, you come to **Calle Oficios,** the most concentrated area of monuments within the centre of Granada. On its higher

Royal Chapel

Granada's most symbolic Christian monument was promoted by the Catholic Monarchs in 1504 so that it would be their mausoleum. In this way they expressed their liking for the city that formed the most valuable of their conquests. The main part of this single-nave

Sepulchre of Felipe and Juana. Royal Chapel.

Interior doorway of the Royal Chapel in the Cathedral.

Nave and grille of the Royal Chapel.

Merchants' Exchange and crowning of the Royal Chalpel.

temple with side chapels was built between 1505 and 1517 under the direction of Enrique Egas in late Gothic or Isabelline style. Until its completion in 1521, the year in which it received the remains of the monarchs from the Alhambra, Plateresque elements were included, and in 1527 García de Pradas crowned the Renaissance façade. In 1518 the **Lonja de Mercaderes** was attached to it, a Gothic-Plateresque building with a façade of superimposed galleries that was the merchants' trade house, today used for the visit to the Royal Chapel. The whole complex is adorned with the exquisite stonework of ornamental tops, vaults and heraldic signs based on the dynastic coat of arms with the eagle of Saint John, the initials F and Y of the sovereigns, the motto, "tanto monta" (so much) and the emblem of the yoke and arrows that symbolised the equality between the king and queen and the union of the kingdoms of Spain.

In the rooms of the Lonja one can appreciate the coffered ceilings, paintings and objects that recall the conquests of the monarchs as a preamble to the route through their funerary chapel and their artistic treasures. In the first section there are several chapels, such as that of the Holy Cross, with carvings by José Risueño from the 18th century. A masterpiece of 16th-century Spanish grille work forged by Bartolomé de Jaén protects the transept, where the sumptuous Renaissance **mausoleums** lie of the Catholic Monarchs and of Felipe the Handsome and Juana the Mad, sculpted in Genoa in Carrara marble, both with reclining effigies of the deceased and a varied iconography of heraldic signs, saints, tro-

Façade of Cathedral in Plaza de las Pasiegas.

phies, personifications and fantastic beings. That of the Catholic Monarchs was carved by Domenico Fancelli in 1517, and of their successors by Bartolomé Ordóñez and Pietro de Carona, in 1519. The lustre of the sepulchre contrasts with the simplicity of the **crypt** situated below, where the lead coffins of the kings and princes lay unadorned.

Two Baroque altarpieces mark out the way towards the head and the sculpted **high altar,** one of the largest Plateresque altarpieces in Spain, produced by Felipe de Bigarny in 1522. Of special note is the relief work on the lower part with scenes of the surrender of Granada and the baptism of the Moriscos, the Moors who converted to Christianity. The most personal legacy of the monarchs is on show in the **sacristy-museum.** It houses the sceptre and crown alongside the royal standard, items from Isabella's dowry, books, silverware and liturgical vestments. Without doubt, the most impressive part is the queen's private collection of paintings, a series of incalculable value made up of Flemish panels by Van der Weyden, Memling and Bouts, oil paintings by Botticelli and

Rear part of the Cathedral.

Chatedral organs.

Perugino, and Spanish masters such as Berruguete.

Cathedral

The Royal Chapel is juxtaposed and directly linked, by means of an inner porch, to the church-cathedral of the Encarnación, the more than 50-metre tower of which signals the heart of the lower part of the city. Construction on it began following the Gothic project of Enrique Egas, but when Diego de Siloe took over the works in 1528, he adapted the work to Renaissance taste, resulting in a building of a classical line with Gothic echoes that, despite opening for worship in 1561, was still subjected to important interventions. On these lines, whereas on the north side the magnificent Renaissance **door of Perdón** opens up, sculpted by Siloe in 1537, before the Plaza de las Pasiegas stands the great Baroque **façade**

designed in 1667 by Alonso Cano. The final completion of the cathedral precinct would not be realised until as late as 1704. The temple has a basilica ground plan with five naves, side chapels and main chapel with an ambulatory at the head. The massive pillars and plain ribbed vaulting on the inside generate a feeling of unusual amplitude, luminosity and lightness, while the abundant artistic catalogue that it guards makes the cathedral a first-class museum. In the bodies of the **Main chapel,** raised as far as the 45 metres height of the dome, over the altar in the form of a shrine engraved in silver and placed in 1926, one can see the statues of the Catholic Monarchs by Pedro de Mena, busts of Adam and Eve by Alonso Cano, the magnificent series of canvases by the same author about the life of the Virgin (1652-1664) and the stained-glass windows made by craftsmen from the Low countries in the 16th century. The **cathedral museum,** in the old Chapter room, shows the custody of the Corpus Christi, donated by Queen Isabel, gold and silverwork, a painting which is attributed to Leonardo and liturgical ornaments. The Baroque altarpieces overlook the tour around the chapels, such as that of the Virgin of the Antigua, one of the most important chapels; that of the Easter Penitent, with paintings by José de Ribera (siglo XVII), Alonso Cano and one attributed to El Greco, and that of the Virgin of the Angustias, based on

Central nave and high chapel of the Cathedral.

Gotic vault of the Cathedral.

coloured marbles. Standing out between the chapels is the Gothic doorway that leads to the Royal Chapel, and another, this time Renaissance, that leads to the sacristy. Over the mahogany cabinets stands the space housing the image of the *Immaculate Conception,* a masterpiece by Alonso Cano dated 1656, and a *Crucifixion* by Martínez Montañés.

The Sagrario and the environs of the Cathedral

Facing the cathedral the severe lines of the church of the Sagrario are drawn, built over the site of the main mosque after its last vestiges had been demolished at the beginning of the 18th century. José de Bada directed the building work of this church with a Greek cross ground plan, in a contained and serious Baroque

Church of the Sagrario.

ALONSO CANO

One of the most notable and multifaceted of Granada's artists, Alonso Cano (1601-1667) did his apprenticeship in Seville with Velasquez and Martínez Montañés, and after a life filled with events – he was accused of murdering his second wife –, he ended up in Granada as a clergyman in the cathedral, for which he made architectural designs and many of his most outstanding paintings and sculptures.

style where the special effects of its vaults and dome are the dominating feature. Then comes the series of religious institutions completed with the Episcopal Palace (17th-19th centuries) and the **Ecclesiastical Curia** (16th century), a Plateresque-style building where Charles V founded the first university of Granada. Before such monumental density, the environs of the cathedral are slightly sweetened by the lively atmosphere of the neighbouring squares and streets. The **Plaza de las Pasiegas** is a Baroque setting with the main façade of the cathedral and its houses with painted walls; behind it the **Plaza de la Pescadería** bustles with the atmosphere of food shops, bars and restaurants, like the neighbouring **Plaza de la Romanilla,** with its watchmen, and that of San Agustín, with the food market, while the spice stalls overwhelm with their aroma and colour in Calle Cárcel Baja which borders the side of the cathedral.

Doorway of the Ecclesiastical Curia.

Plaza de las Pasiegas with the Cathedral and the Curia.

Towards San Jerónimo
and the Cartuja

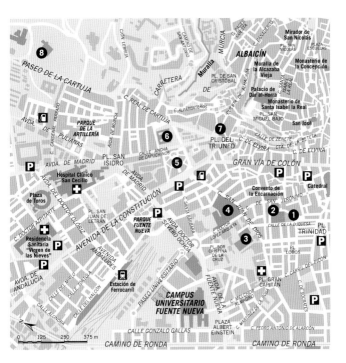

1. Botanical Gardens
2. Church of the Santos Justo y Pastor
3. Monastery of San Jerónimo
4. Hospital and church of San Juan de Dios
5. Jardines del Triunfo
6. Hospital Real
7. Puerta de Elvira
8. The Cartuja

Hospital of San Juan de Dios. Cloister.

Caicedo Palace.

The residential areas spread from the centre to the best, some of them older, forming a draught-board of squares and still narrow streets, and others, more modern and laid out in wide avenues and enlargements that reach the outskirts. It is a modern area full of life in which, nevertheless, as is the case for all of Granada, there are many historical and monumental reference points, of a scale as formidable as San Jerónimo or of such inner refinement as the Cartuja.

From the Trinidad to San Jerónimo

Still within the shadows of the cathedral and the city centre, the **Plaza de la Trinidad** gathers the commercial hustle and bustle of Calle Mesones and Calle Alhóndiga and creates a quiet corner in the shadows of the trees. It is a good starting point for the walk to the **Botanical Garden** and the **Plaza de la Universidad,** a boiling pot of young people – the student population of Granada is very high indeed, which has a knock-on effect on its pace of life – before the old Jesuit college of San Pablo, today a university faculty, and the **church of the Santos Justo y Pastor** (16th-18th centuries), which feature among the richest in the city due to their artistic heritage, with sculptures by Alonso de Mena and José de Mora. From here, on passing palaces such as those of Caicedo or Ansoti, Calle Gran Capitán is reached, the central street of this sector, and the monastery of San Jerónimo.

Monastery of San Jerónimo

The well-built volume of San Jerónimo stands out as one of the most dominant reminders of the Castilian conquerors, and it is no coincidence that the monastery was linked to "Gonzalo

Monastery of San Jerónimo.

Fernández of Cordoba, great captain of the Spanish, terror of the French and Turks", as a console has inscribed at the head of the church, where his remains lie. Promoted by the Catholic Monarchs, work began on it in 1519 in Gothic style, being adapted to Renaissance norms when Jacopo Florentino and Diego de Siloe took over the continuation of the work in 1525. The immense grandeur of the whole imposes itself from the same spot: it is the impression given by the façade of the **church,** with a classical doorway and royal emblems at the foot of a four-bodied tower, a feeling that increases on the inside before its spacious Gothic nave covered with fresco paintings and the architecture of the transept and head, with powerful stone vaults carved with dozens of relief work pieces over the largest sculptural **altarpiece** in Spanish

Renaissance work, produced from 1570 by first-class craftsmen such as Juan Bautista Vázquez, Pablo de Rojas or Martínez Montañés. The monastic rooms are arranged around two **cloisters,** the smallest dating from 1520 and reserved today for the cloistered nuns, and the other of much more consider-

Church of San Jerónimo.

able size, attached to the church, which provides an excellent example of Isabelline Gothic, with a garden, robust arcades and rooms that exhibit interesting pieces of artwork.

San Juan de Dios and the Triunfo

Close to San Jerónimo is the **hospital and church of San Juan de Dios,** the main centre of the order created by the legendary Juan Ciudad – later Saint John of God – who, after an adventurous life, gave himself entirely to caring for the sick. It comprises two arcaded courtyards from the 17th and 18th centuries and a totally Baroque church that was completed in 1759 by José de Bada. A startling doorway with sculptures between two towers leads to the inside full of paintings and relief work with a churrigueresque high altar and

Triunfo Gardens.

the luxurious chapel where the saint's remains are kept. Calle San Juan de Dios rises until it meets with Gran Vía and Avenida de la Constitución, an unceasing traffic point before the **Triunfo Gardens,** the sloping area of ground marked out by the monument in honour of the Immaculate

Hospital of San Juan de Dios. Cloister.

Hospital Real. Portada

Conception (17th century). In the higher part is the **Hospital Real** and at the foot of the Albaicin, the square with the **Puerta de Elvira,** one of the oldest and largest entrance gates to the Arab city (11th-14th centuries), at the end of the street with the same name. From the Triunfo, the historic quarter opens up to the areas of modern expansion where, surviving as a memory of the past in the middle of the university campus, is the old convent of the Cartuja, at the end of Calle Real de Cartuja and the Paseo de la Cartuja.

The Cartuja

Granada's overwhelming artistic imagination once again impresses us in this old monastery placed on the spot known by the poetic Arab name of *Aynadamar* – "source of tears" –, famous in its time for its orchards and houses of leisure.

Constituted in 1513, after three centuries it became one of the most sumptuous monastic centres in the city, the outer austerity barely concealing the verve of the inside. The area is made up of the church and the annexed **cloister**, the only survivor of several that it once had. The galleries of columns surround the garden from where the different chapels and rooms are reached that correspond to the earliest constructions of the convent. Here one can admire a meticulous series of paintings dating from the early 17th century, the majority of them from the brush of Friar Juan Sánchez Cotán. The Profundis Room and the refectory deserve special attention for the effects given off by their walls. In the **church,** the air of recollection is transformed into an outrageous deployment of Baroque style. The temple (16th-18th centuries)

Cloister of the Mármoles of the Hospital Real.

HOSPITAL REAL

This noble building, raised over the Triunfo, was founded by the Catholic Monarchs in 1504 as part of the institutional programme they undertook after the conquest. Today belonging to the university, it is made up of a large square with cross naves that separate four courtyards, showing a superimposition of styles that reflect the time span of the work from 1511 until the early 17th century from an initial design project by Enrique Egas. Along with Gothic and Renaissance elements, such as the graceful Cloister of the Mármoles by Diego de Siloe, it has a Baroque doorway dating from 1632.

is adorned with relief work in plaster, marbles, wood, frescos, oils, sculptures and a baldachin of gilded wood. The paroxysm reaches its height with the **Sancta Sanctorum,** a unique Baroque piece made by Francisco Hurtado Izquierdo completed in 1720 in which architecture, painting and sculpture are combined in an abundance of daring fantasy beneath the bright dome illuminated by Antonio Palomino. The baroque apotheosis of the Cartuja continues in the **Sacristy,** a composition without precedent that was begun in 1732 and also attributed to Hurtado Izquierdo where the play of light and shade of the multicoloured plasterwork is enriched with magnificent sculptures and lustrous mahogany, ebony, nacre, silver and marble cabinets.

Sacristy of the Cartuja.

Doorway and church of the Cartuja.

Around the Realejo and the Genil

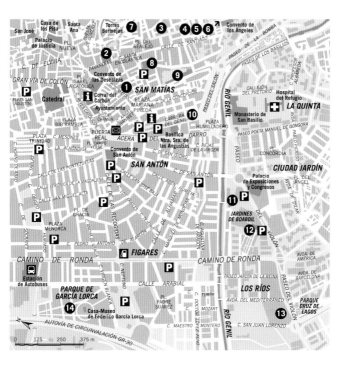

1. Parish of San Matías
2. Casa de los Tiros
3. Campo del Príncipe
4. La Antequeruela
5. Carmen de los Mártires
6. Casa de Manuel de Falla
7. Villa of the Foundation Rodríguez Acosta

8. Church of Santo Domingo
9. Cuarto Real de Santo Domingo
10. Carrera del Genil
11. Ermita de San Sebastián
12. Alcázar Genil
13. Science Park
14. Huerta de San Vicente

The centre, the Alhambra hill and the Genil shape one of the most traditional parts of Granada. The districts of San Matías, the Realejo, the Antequeruela, site of the early Jewish settlement that spread its name of *Garnata* to the rest of the city, later a suburb of the Alfareros whereby the number of houses of leisure of the Muslim aristocracy grew, and later still a Christian area populated by many churches, convents and palaces. These districts look out to the passageways of the Genil, which in its descent to the Vega crosses an increasingly modern setting.

The Realejo

From the Plaza de Isabel la Católica, Calle Pavaneras winds its way towards the Realejo. At the beginning, on the right, Calle de San Matías drops, the nerve centre of the popular district that is home to the convent of the Carmelitas Descalzas, founded in 1582 in the houses of the Gran Capitán, and the parish church of **San Matías,** with Renaissance doorways concluded in 1550. Again along Calle Pavaneras the presence of historic buildings intensifies with the Casa de Padre Suárez (16th century), where the illustrious Jesuit philosopher was born, and the Casa de los Tiros, a small fortified palace built between 1510 and 1540 which got its name for the muskets, or "tiros", shots, imbedded in the façade. The masonry front with battlements features mythological sculptures (Hercules, Jason…) and above the entrance, the curious hieroglyphic – "the heart commands" – used as the motto for the Granada Venegas family, one of the Nasrid lineages integrated into the Castilian nobility after the conquest. The inside, the home today of the museum of the history of the city, features the Golden Hall, covered by a ceiling with

CASA DE LOS TIROS MUSEUM
The rooms of its three floors provide a tour of the romantic image and representations of the city through a wide-ranging repertoire of illustrations, oil paintings, watercolours, portraits of Granada figures, period photographs, posters, documents, forms and newspapers, recreations of settings and items of popular culture, such as textiles, dishes and ceramic figures and a great diversity of objects.

Cristo de los Favores and Campo del Príncipe.

portraits and legends of Spanish heroes and noblemen. Other mansions line the walk to the Plaza del Realejo, the crossroads and traditional marketplace of the district, and the **Campo del Príncipe,** the most popular and busiest meeting place, a wide level area with an infinite number of tapas bars overlooked by the Cristo de los Favores, one of the images that arouses most fervour amongst the people of Granada, placed here in 1682. At three o'clock in the afternoon on Good Friday worshippers gather here to pray and ask for three favours, of which, they say, one is always granted.

The Antequeruela

Over the Campo del Príncipe staggers the **Antequeruela,** the district that housed the Muslims expelled from the city of Antequera after its conquest by the Castilians in 1410. At the foot of the slope the church dedicated to the patron saint of Granada, Saint Cecilius, stands out, with a Plateresque doorway, built in the first third of the 16th century over a mosque. Continuing uphill the slopes on the edge of the Alhambra wood spread out, an area of great beauty with magnificent views such as those provided by the terrace of the Alhambra Palace hotel, whose exotic Moorish architecture has the appearance of a film set. Around here one can also visit several of the *cármenes,* the traditional houses with walled gardens, most noted for their beauty and history. On the crest of the hill, on the site of the Carmelite convent where Saint John of the Cross lived and was inspired, is the **Carmen de los Mártires,** a small palace dating from the mid-19th century surrounded by romantic gardens with ponds, sculptures, melancholic craftsmen's ruins,

Auditorium Manuel de Falla.

and the splendid view over the city and the Vega at its feet. Close by is the **house of Manuel de Falla** and, in the narrow Calle de los Niños del Royo, the **walled house of the Fundación Rodríguez Acosta.** Just as appreciable as the building itself – an exquisite modernist composition between cypresses completed in 1930 –

HOUSE-MUSEUM OF MANUEL DE FALLA
Calle Antequeruela Alta hosts the quiet walled house where Manuel de Falla (1876-1946) lived, considered the most important Spanish composer in the 20th century. Born in Cádiz, de Falla, was great friends with Lorca, lived in Granada between 1921 and 1939, when he went into exile in Argentina. The house retains the atmosphere of the years during which it was the artist's home, with the period objects and a large collection of documents and personal objects.

are the museum's collections which include: archaeology, sculpture and, above all, early 20th-century paintings. Going down the hillside, in the shadow of the Bermejas Towers, the steep **district of Mauror** branches out like a smaller version of the Albaicin, a redoubt of the old Jewish quarter with corners such as the convent of Santa Catalina de Siena, established in 1530, or the Puerta del Sol, with an old public wash house.

Towards the Carrera and the walks around the Genil

The Realejo slope returns to the low centre of the district and its setting of palaces and convents. Calle Santiago is notable for the Comendadoras de Santiago (16th-18th centuries) and in the adjoining square the monument in honour of the theologian Friar Luis de Granada, the **church of Santo Domingo** and the convent of Santa Cruz la Real, one of the Catholic Monarchs' first foundations after the conquest, built between the 16th and 18th centuries over the orchards of the Almanjarra. The temple combines Plateresque and Gothic elements, such as the portico of the façade and the interior vaults, with the spectacular Baroque chapel of the Virgin of the Rosary added in the 18th century. Beside this stands the Islamic jewel of the **Royal Hall of Santo Domingo,** a 13th-century tower-cum-palace used as a

Church of Santo Domingo.

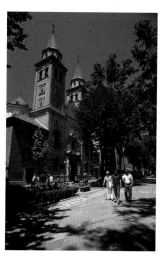

Basilica of Nuestra Señora de las Angustias.

retreat by the Nasrid sultans with an orchard and an incredibly rich room with plasterwork and tiling beneath a wooden framework.

The outer edges of the Realejo end with the **Plaza de la Mariana** – or de Mariana Pineda – and the **Campillo Bajo,** the popular square alongside the Bibataubín Palace (18th century), the home of the Provincial Council, and the extension that links Puerta Real with the **Carrera del Genil.** In this tree-lined straight way, a favourite for strolling, stand the twin towers of the **basilica of Nuestra Señora de las Angustias,** the patron saint, built at the end of the 17th century. The inside, full of excellent sculptures and paintings, houses a

MARIANA PINEDA

One of Granada's most popular figures is Mariana Pineda (1804-1831), the romantic heroine famous for the strength of character with which she faced her deadly fate. In the death rattles of the absolutism of Ferdinand VII she played an active role in the political conspiracies and, on being discovered with a liberal flag that she herself had embroidered and refusing to name her fellow-conspirators, she was led to the gallows in the prime of her youth.

Bridge over the River Genil.

Downriver the vegetation extends along the **Paseo del Violón** facing the modern structures of the Exhibition and Congress Hall. Its size and shape contrast with two small Islamic monuments situated close by: the **hermitage of San Sebastián,** an old 13th-century Muslim murabit or oratory, and the **Alcázar Genil,** a leisure pavilion of the Nasrid royal family built in the 14th century.

Science Park and Huerta de San Vicente

Modernity imposes itself when the Genil reaches the modern area of urban expansion towards the south. The most recent evidence of this is the very large head offices of the Caja Granada bank, by the architect Campo Baeza, in the Carretera de la Armilla, while alongside the river, on the other side of the Camino de Ronda, the **Science park,** opened in 1995,

marble altarpiece and the sparkling Baroque chapel in which the image of the Virgin is venerated. At the end of the Carrera del Genil one can take in the deep breath of freshness from the gardens that accompany the river's course, the **Paseo del Salón** and its continuation, the **Paseo de la Bomba.**

Paseo del Salón, on the shores of the river.

represents a real landmark with its geometric volumes and domes. In terms of both its buildings and conception, this innovative contemporary setting is an invitation to take an active part through interactive mediums and audiovisual supports. Its contents are dedicated to science, the universe and perception by means of thematic installations regarding the biosphere, light, sound and energy, along with a planetarium, an astronomic garden with solar clocks and calendars, a butterfly park with tropical species and sections about the scientific legacy of Al-Andalus and the network of protected natural spaces in Andalusia, the largest land area in Spain. The itinerary ends in the city outskirts. From the Science Park Calle Arabial leads to the García Lorca Park, the large gardened area that envelops **Huerta de San Vicente,** the house in which Federico García Lorca

FEDERICO GARCÍA LORCA

Born in Fuente Vaqueros, a village of farmers on the fertile plain just outside Granada, Federico García Lorca (1898-1936) was one of the most important figures of Spanish culture in the 20th century and one of the artists who has aroused the greatest interest at an international level. His untiring creativity was expressed in an enormous flow of literary, poetic and above all dramatic works, and of other artistic disciplines, such as stage design or music.

spent the summers and some of his finest moments between 1926 and 1936, when he left here, never to return. The rooms, with the original furnishings, manuscripts, drawings, photos and documents set the scene where the artist wrote some of his most famous pieces of work, such as the drama *Bodas de Sangre.*

Science Park.

Huerta de San Vicente.

Excursions around the province

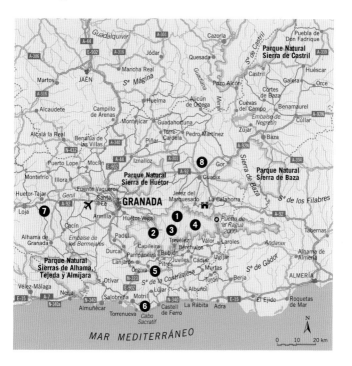

1. Sierra Nevada
2. Pico del Veleta
3. Mulhacén
4. Sierra Nevada National Park
5. The Alpujarra
6. The Costa Tropical
7. La Vega and El Poniente
8. Guadix and the Marquesado

Sierra Nevada.

Sierra Nevada.

Sierra Nevada

The diversity of the land of Granada is to a large extent due to Sierra Nevada, the legendary *Solair* – or "mountain of the Sun" – of the Muslims, which crosses a large part of the province and climbs above 3,000 metres just 30 kilometres from the capital, revealing an amazing variety of landscapes that range from the cultivated valleys and wooded slopes to the meadows and constant snowy peaks of the high mountain. From the Granada bypass or the avenues alongside the Genil an easy road is taken (A-395) that rises above the river and climbs up the massive mountainous area revealing expansive panoramic views of Granada and its environs. It leads to **Pradollano,** at 2,100 metres altitude, the centre of the most southerly ski resort in Europe, with all the facilities required for a stay and doing winter sports and other activities, such as trekking. Climbing further up, the asphalted road continues through the enclave of **Borreguiles** until reaching **Veleta,** at 3,392 m, the second highest point of the mas-

---

SIERRA NEVADA NATIONAL PARK

The scenery, vegetation and fauna of Sierra Nevada were the reasons behind its declaration as a Biosphere Reserve in 1986, Natural Park in 1989 and National Park in 1999, currently comprising more than 170,000 hectares of protected land. Its most sensitive area is concentrated around the peaks of Mulhacén and Veleta. Special interest lies in its botanical richness, with 2,100 species of flower out of the 8,000 present on the peninsula and 66 exclusive species. The centre in Dornajo, after 23 km of the Sierra Nevada road, provides all one needs for the visit.

The Alpujarra. Barranco del Poqueira.

sif, hanging over impressive ravines, from which one can make out a fantastic setting of crests, crags, glacial cirques and lagoons, and as many as sixteen peaks that exceed 3,000 m, headed by **Mulhacén,** the mountain named in honour of the sultan Muley Hassan, who commanded that he be buried on its peak, which, at 3,482 m, marks the rooftop of the peninsula.

The Alpujarra

The Alpujarra of Granada covers the southern slope of Sierra Nevada as it drops towards the Mediterranean. Its titanic mountainous geography gives it a unique character, emphasised by a history of singular traditions. The county experienced its splendour with the Muslims thanks to silk and a flourishing agriculture on irrigated land, later becoming the last refuge of the Moorish people, where they resisted until their final defeat after the uprising of 1568. Today its popular culture is still shown in its architecture, in the festivals of Moors and Christians, in a succulent gastronomy and in the strength of its craftsmanship. **Lanjarón** (45 km away via the A-44 and A-348),

The Alpujarra.

Salobreña, between sugar cane plantations.

the town of spas and crystal-clear waters, is the western gateway to the Alpujarra, halfway up the hillside before the ruins of an Arab castle. Very close by is **Órgiva,** in the heart of the valley amid fruit trees and olive groves on the banks of the Guadalfeo. The twin towers of its parish church and the castle-cum-palace of the Counts of Sástago mark the town centre of this crossroads and major town in the county. From here the winding GR-421 road climbs up in the **high Alpujarra** and leads to the Poqueira ravine, where the cluster of delightful whitewashed villages that make up **Pampaneira, Bubión** and **Capileira** provide one of the most enticing views in the region. This is where the most characteristic traits of the Alpujarra can be savoured to the full: Mudejar churches alongside squares from which narrow and steep streets branch off in a

rural atmosphere that seems to be trapped in time, magnificent views over hillocks with oak and chestnut woods or worked into terraces for agriculture, immense landscapes with the sea in the distance as the road extends forward in the direction of **Pitres, Pórtugos,** with its famous Fuente Agria spring, and **Busquístar,** until **Trevélez,** the highest town in Spain, at the foot of the Mulhacén peak, that spreads out over its three districts – Alto, Medio y Bajo (high, middle and low) – from 1,600 metres. Trevélez is also famous for its hams cured by the cold mountain air. Another extensive stretch of the high Alpujarra reaches out to the east before the border with Almería, a lessvisited part through a trail of equally substantial villages: **Juviles, Mecina Bombarón, Yegen** and **Válor,** birthplace of the Moorish chief Ibn Umayya,

Beaches of Almuñécar.

and **Laroles,** the entrance to the Puerto de la Ragua, the only pass that crosses the range. From here the road descends to the valleys of the eastern Alpujarra where there are two large towns, **Ugíjar** and **Cádiar,** which, alongside the A-348, closes the circuit by the Guadalfeo valley in the direction of Órgiva.

The Costa Tropical

Few places in Spain experience such emphatic contrasts as in Granada. Just 40 km separate the alpine meadows of Sierra Nevada from the beaches and coves of transparent water of the quality of Almuñécar, Salobreña and Motril, a stretch of the Mediterranean coastline which, due to its benign climate, has earned it the name of Costa Tropical.

    Salobreña (65 km away, via the A-44 and N-323), the first

town the traveller comes across arriving from Granada, represents the perfect model of white town forming a cluster of whitewashed houses over a crag with an Arab fortress overlooking the sea. Towards the west via the N-340 appear the beaches and urbanisations of **Almuñécar,** one of the

La Herradura. Almuñécar.

Santa Fe. Granada Doorway.

main tourist centres along the
Granada coast. Founded by the
Phoenicians and called Sexi in
Antiquity, Almuñécar possesses an
interesting historic quarter at the
foot of the castle of San Miguel
and is surrounded by cliffs and
tempting beaches, such as **the
Herradura,** and valleys with exotic
fruit plantations such as avocado
and custard apple. Towards the
east, also alongside the N-340, is
Motril, the second biggest town of
the province, bordering the sugar-
cane fields and fruit orchards and
nearby a coastal area where its
commercial port is situated as
are the busy developments of
Torrenueva or **Castell de Ferro,**
continuing towards Almería, at
the foot of the Contraviesa
range, along a series of fishing
and holiday villages – La Mamola,
Melicena, La Rábita... – among
lighthouses and old watchtowers.

La Vega and El Poniente

At the gateways of Granada
spreads the rich lowland area of
the Genil, the fertile plain that is
becoming increasingly absorbed
into the greater metropolitan area
of the capital. It is the perfect
area for escaping to, to spend a
short while in a country inn or tour
its villages, which provide no end
of interest. This is the case of
Santa Fe (11 km away, via the
A-92), founded by the Catholic
Monarchs as an encampment
from where the final conquest of
Granada was organised. In fact,
it is here where the surrender of
the Nasrid capital was signed
and, in 1492, the Capitulations
with Christopher Columbus with
which he gained the support of
the Crown for his journey of discovery. The historic quarter still
preserves the layout of its origins,
with a square overlooked by the
Royal House and the massive neo-

Fuente Vaqueros. Birthplace of F. García Lorca.

Fortress of Moclín.

classical church built in 1785. Also among the poplar groves and irrigation channels of the Vega is the country town of **Fuente Vaqueros** (17 km away), birthplace of Federico García Lorca: the visit to the house where he was born shows the poet's family atmosphere and aspects of his life and work. La Vega is closed off by the line of mountains of Granada's west, El Poniente, and the towns that formed the last frontier between Muslims and Christians. Like a medieval engraving, **Moclín** (33 km away, off a turning of the N-432) stands out among the mountainous scenery at the foot of a solid Nasrid fortress. Further on appears the romantic image of **Montefrío** (50 km away via the A-335), a particularly beautiful village in the shadows of the dizzying cliff crowned by the Renaissance church of the town.

On the edge of the A-92 and of the Genil lies **Loja** (54 km away), on the mountainous pass where the Vega begins, the reason behind why its called the "key of Granada". Its streets slide down the Islamic Alcazaba scattered with churches such as that of San Gabriel (16th century) and

Montefrío.

Alhama de Granada.

town – its conquest announced the end of Nasrid Granada – with an attractive country house in which the church of the Encarnación (16th century) is noteworthy. The outskirts also host the renowned thermal spa, with rooms dating from the Al-Andalus period, to which Alhama owes its name, from *al-hamman,* the baths.

Guadix and the Marquesado

Just 60 km along the A-92 in the direction of Almería one reaches one of the most unknown counties in the Andalusian region, the maze of gullies, valleys and high plateaus that are found around **Guadix.** On the way one crosses the **Natural Park of the Sierra de Huétor,** one of the favourite relaxation spots of the people of Granada. A spectacular geological setting begins further on of clayey soils beneath the north face of

fountains such as that of the Veinticinco Caños (twenty-five spouts). On a plateau alongside the **Natural Park of the Alhama, Tejeda and Almijara** ranges is **Alhama de Granada** (58 km Hawai via the A-335), raised on the projection that the narrow passes cut out of its river. A small romantic

Guadix. Arab Alcazaba.

Castle of La Calahorra.

Sierra Nevada, the vast horizon of high moors, ravines and orchards in sight of **Guadix,** the capital of Granada's eastern part. In this very old city our attention is drawn to the Cathedral (16th-18th centuries), with a Gothic-Renaissance interior and a magnificent Baroque façade, the arcaded Plaza Mayor, the Islamic Alcazaba (11th century) and the fascinating district of cave houses that blend in with the terrain. The foot of the range shelters a cluster of villages of the **Marquesado del Zenete,** notable for their popular architecture and the overwhelming presence of **the castle of La Calahorra,** the fortress completed in 1512 whose artistic courtyard is considered a key work of the Spanish renaissance. Climbing the hill, the **Puerto de la Ragua,** with a small winter resort between woods, provides us with the opportunity to enjoy Sierra Nevada from a different viewpoint. A pleasant surprise still awaits us to the north of the province in the city of **Baza** and its range, Galera with its caves, the high plateaus of Orce, Huéscar and Puebla de Don Fadrique, and the Natural Park of the Sierra de Castril.

Guadix. District of the house caves.

Practical guide

LEISURE

FESTIVALS

The vitality of Granada's traditions can be seen from its varied festival calendar, with celebrations with historical, religious or secular origins.

Día de la Toma (day of the conquest) 2nd of January. The commemoration of the entry of the Catholic Monarchs in 1492 is the most singular anniversary event in Granada. After the beginning of the acts in the Royal Chapel and civic-religious procession, the rite of flaunting the standard of the monarchs from the balcony of the Town hall takes place, in the Plaza del Carmen.

Cavalcade of the Three Kings of the Orient

5th of January. It dates from the late 19th century and is the oldest in Spain. The procession of horses, camels and floats goes through the main streets of the city, from the Avenida de la Constitución to the Genil, until reaching the Plaza del Carmen.

Andalusia Day

28th of February, the festival of the Autonomous Community.

Festival and pilgrimage of Saint Cecilius

The 2nd and the first Sunday in February. The festival of the patron saint of Granada is held with religious acts and a pilgrimage to the Abbey of Sacromonte to visit its catacombs and to spend a day in the country.

Carnival

Early February.
The increasingly popular festival livened up by the revelry of the dance groups and humorous musical bands.

Easter

March or April. From Palm Sunday until the Resurrection, more than thirty associations parade through the streets staging one of the most spectacular Easter celebrations in Andalusia. The processions carry very heavy floats with statues of great value, exhibiting a magnificent repertoire from the Granada school of religious images dating from the 16th to 18th centuries, often to the rhythm of the saetas, flamenco-style sacred songs. The processions stop before the cathedral for acts of penitence and make up a vibrant sight through the districts of the old quarter, from the Carrera del Darro or the Albaicín to the Alhambra and the Sacromonte, where fires are lit when the Christ of the Gypsies pases on Ash Wednesday.

Crosses of May

From the 3rd of May. The festive events take place around the crosses and altars that are raised in the popular districts, such as the Albaicín or the Realejo.

Civic Festival of Mariana Pineda

Around the 26th of May. Diverse acts in the Plaza del Ayuntamiento in memory of Granada's liberal heroine.

Fair and festival of the Corpus Christi

End of May and beginning of June. Granada's big festival. The fair begins the Saturday before Corpus Christi Thursday in the area of stalls and attractions that is assembled on the outskirts, next to the Jaén road. Wednesday sees the procession with the Tarasca — the roaring dragon trodden on by a woman —, devils, giants and 'bigheads', and on Thursday, the solemn religious procession with the silver monstrance that leaves from the cathedral. The fair, accompanied by bullfighting and other festivities, finishes on the Sunday.

Patron saint festivals of the Virgin of the Angustias

The 15th and last Sunday in September. A floral offering is made on the 15th to the basilica of the patron saint, and on the Sunday, a well-attended procession, while in the Carrera de la Virgen stalls are set up with fresh fruit and traditional produce.

Saint Michael

28th of September. Festival of the Albaicín district, with a lively pilgrimage to the hermitage of the hill of San Miguel.

New Year's Eve

31st of December. People meet in front of the Town hall clock in the Plaza del Carmen.

MUSEUMS

Alhambra
Tel. 958 22 75 25
www.alhambra-patronato.es
Tickets Tel. 902 22 44 60
www.alhambratickets.com

Hams from Alpujarra.

SKIING IN SIERRA NEVADA
Just 30 km from Granada along a good road is the ski resort of Sierra Nevada, the southernmost ski resort in Europe. Visitors have the opportunity to do winter sports with all the added facilities of accommodation, restaurants, bars, shops, equipment hire, beginners' classes with instructors, ice skating, heated pools, etc. The resort has nearly 80 ski slopes, more than twenty ski lifts, chair lifts and cable-cars. The skiing season is from early December to the end of April. During the rest of the year it is possible to do other outdoor sports such as trekking, cycling or adventure sports.
Sierra Nevada Ski Resort. Plaza de Andalucía.
Tel. 958 24 91 00 / 902 70 80 90. www.cetursa.es

Federico García Lorca House-Museum
Huerta de San Vicente
Calle Virgen Blanca, s/n
Tel. 958 25 84 66
www.huertadesanvicente.com
Manuel de Falla House-Museum
Calle Antequeruela Alta, 11
Tel. 958 22 21 88
www.museomanueldefalla.com
José Guerrero Centre
Calle Oficios, 8
Tel. 958 22 51 85
www.centroguerrero.org
Fundación Rodríguez-Acosta
Callejón Niños del Rollo, 9
Tel. 958 22 74 97. www.fundaciorodriguezacosta.com
Museum of the Alhambra
Historical monument centre of the Alhambra. Palace of Charles V.

Tel. 958 02 79 00
www.alhambra-patronato.es
Archaeological and Ethnological museum of Granada
Carrera del Darro, 41-43
Tel. 958 22 56 03. www.juntadeandalucia.es/cultura/museoarqueologicogranada
Fine Arts Museum of Granada
Historical monument centre

of the Alhambra. Palace of Charles V. Tel. 958 22 14 49
www.juntadeandalucia.es/cultura/museobellasartesgranada
Casa de los Tiros Museum
Calle Pavaneras, 19
Tel. 958 22 10 72
www.juntadeandalucia.es/cultura/museocasadelostiros
San Juan de Dios Museum
(Saint John of God)
Casa de los Pisa.
Calle Convalecencia, 1
Tel. 958 22 21 44
www.sanjuandedios-oh.es
Science Park
Avenida del Mediterráneo, s/n
Tel. 958 13 19 00
www.parqueciencias.com

SHOW VENUES
Manuel de Falla Auditorium
Classical music. Headquarters of the Granada City Orchestra.
Paseo de los Mártires, s/n
Tel. 958 22 00 22
Alhambra Theatre
Calle Molinos, 56
Tel. 958 02 80 00
Isabel la Católica Theatre
Main venue for stage arts and music in Granada. Close to the Casino. Tel. 902 40 02 22 / 958 22 29 07
Municipal theatre of Zaidín
Calle Andrés Segovia, 60
Tel. 958 12 54 10
Granada International Festival of Music and Dance.
This leading festival takes place between the end of

La Alhambra.

June and early July with a programme that includes a wide range of artistic events – symphonic orchestra concerts, dance and ballet, recitals, chamber music, all-night flamenco concerts… – in venues all around the main monuments and all over the city, such as the Palace of Charles V, the Comares Palace, the gardens of the Generalife, the Cartuja or the Sacromonte, among others.
Calle San Jerónimo, 5
Tel. 958 22 18 44
www.granadafestival.org

GRANADA WITH CHILDREN

As well as the areas with

Museo Arqueológico. Casa de Castril.

historic buildings such as the Alhambra or the Generalife, there are some particularly good spots for spending time with the children, such as the García Lorca Park, which has children's facilities, or the walks along the Genil. The attrac-

tions of the Science Park and the Granada Eye, with a camera obscura, in Calle Cruz de Quirós, 12, are also suitable places for having some fun. Fun is also guaranteed, naturally, on a trip to Sierra Nevada, which can be easily done in a day.

PRACTICAL INFORMATION

TRANSPORT

AIR

Granada Airport
Motorway A-92, Chauchina. (17 km). Tel. 958 24 52 00 / 958 24 52 23. Daily flight connections with Madrid and Barcelona and other national and international connections. As well as taxis, there is a bus service between the airport and the centre of Granada between 8 a.m. and 11 p.m. Journey time is just 30 minutes, and the final destination is the Palacio de Congresos, in the Paseo del Violón. Tel. 958 49 01 64
www.aena.es

TRAIN

Renfe Station
Avenida de los Andaluces, s/n
Tel. 958 24 02 02
All train lines.
Renfe (National Train Network)
Tel. 902 24 02 02
www.renfe.es
www.eltren.com

BUS

Bus Station
Lines to Sierra Nevada, all the province, the rest of Andalusia and other Spanish and international destinations. Different companies according to destination (Alsina Graells, Autedia, Agobe, B. G., Alsa-Enatcar, Bonal)
Carretera de Jaén, s/n
Tel. 958 18 54 80
Local buses
The local bus network has more than twenty lines that cover the whole city. There is a micro-bus service, identifiable with the sign "Alhambra Bus" which, from the Plaza Nueva, runs on the hills of the Alhambra and the Albaicin.
Transportes Rober
Tel. 900 71 09 00
www.trasnportesrober.com

TAXIS

Radio Taxi Genil
Tel. 958 13 23 23

Radio-Taxi Granada
Tel. 958 15 14 61
Tele-Radio-Taxi
Tel. 958 28 06 54
Servi Taxi
958 40 01 99 (Granada area)

USEFUL PHONE NUMBERS

Junta de Andalucía (Regional Government)
Tel. 902 50 55 05
Tourist Offices of the Junta de Andalucía
Calle Santa Ana, 4
Tel. 958 22 59 90
Alhambra
Avenida del Generalife, s/n
Tel. 958 22 95 75
Tourist Office of the Diputación de Granada
(Granada Provincial Council)
Plaza Mariana Pineda, 10
Tel: 958 24 71 28
Granada City Council
Tel. 958 24 81 00
Directory Enquiries
Tel. 11888, 11811

Parador de San Francisco.

Emergency telephone numbers
Tel. 112
Medical emergencies
Tel. 061, 958 28 20 00
Police
Tel. 091 y 092
All-night chemists
Tel. 958 27 17 17

GRANADA ON THE WEB

Web page of the City of Granada Tourist Board
www.granadatur.com
Province of Granada Tourist Board
www.turismodegranada.org
Rural tourism in Granada and its province
www.turgranada.com
Web page of the Andalusian Tourist Board
www.andalucia.org
Portal of the Junta de Andalucía
www.juntadeandalucia.es

ACCOMMODATION

Information and bookings from Turismo Andaluz
Tel. 902 20 00 037
AC Palacio de Santa Paula [★★★★★]
On the main street of the historic centre, it is luxurious, paying attention to detail, modern and at the same time reminiscent of the past, built over an old convent, of which

the cloister and other spaces have been preserved, and a series of Moorish houses. Gran Vía de Colón, 31
Tel. 958 80 57 40
Hospes Palacio de los Patos [★★★★★]
A small place where the taste for tradition harmonises with futurism and cutting-edge technology. Calle Recogidas, 11. Tel. 958 53 65 16
Parador de San Francisco [★★★★]
It occupies an old convent, built in its time over one of the Nasrid palaces of the Alhambra, of which some remains are preserved. Pleasant, evocative of the past, a magnificent property in an unbeatable setting. Calle Real de la Alhambra, s/n. Tel. 958 22 14 40
Alhambra Palace [★★★★]
Embedded in a slope on the hills of the Alhambra with the city at its feet, it is a legendary hotel due to the exotic Moorish architecture of its building, dating from 1910, and the personalities that have stayed there. Plaza Arquitecto García de Paredes, 1
Tel. 958 22 14 68
Hotel Meliá Granada [★★★★]
In the commercial centre of Granada, quiet and pleasant. Calle Ángel Ganivet, 7
Tel. 958 22 74 00

Hotel Plaza Nueva [★★★★]
In a rehabilitated house with a romantic air, alongside one of the essential focal points of the historic centre of Granada. Plaza Nueva, 2
Tel. 958 21 52 73
Hotel Saray [★★★★]
Very large and cutting-edge design, in a modern area very close to the Palacio de Congresos. Paseo Enrique Tierno Galván, 4
Tel. 958 13 00 09
Carmen de Santa Inés [★★★]
Typical walled house of the Albaicín, with a quiet garden facing the Alhambra. Placeta de Porras, 7
Tel. 958 22 63 80
Casa de Federico [★★★]
A hotel in the new style in a restored house in the centre close to the cathedral. Calle Horno de Marina, 13.
Tel. 958 20 85 34
Casa del Capitel Nazarí [★★★]
16th-century courtyard house, very well cared-for and peaceful, next to Plaza Nueva. Cuesta Aceituneros, 6
Tel. 958 21 52 60
Casa Morisca [★★★]
Old Moorish house in the Albaicín restored with the best taste and all the rooms are different, overlooking the Alhambra. Cuesta de la Victoria, 9
Tel. 958 22 11 00

Bodega Castañeda.

El Ladrón de Agua [★★★]
16th-century mansion rehabilitated with perfect touches
of modernity, at the foot of
the Albaicin.
Carrera del Darro, 13
Tel. 958 21 50 40

Hotel Reina Cristina [★★★]
19th-century building, next to
the Plaza de la Trinidad and
close to the cathedral. It was
the home of the Rosales family where Lorca was arrested.
Calle Tablas, 4
Tel. 958 25 32 11

Los Tilos [★★]
In one of the cosiest and
most pleasant squares in the
centre. Plaza Bibarrambla, 4
Tel. 958 26 67 12

Maciá Plaza [★★]
Very well placed in the
historic centre.
Plaza Nueva, 4
Tel. 958 22 75 36

Hotel América [★]
Of undoubted charm due to
its chosen location in the
Alhambra.
Calle Real de la Alhambra, 53
Tel. 958 22 74 71

Youth Hostel
Calle Ramón y Cajal, 2
Tel. 958 00 29 00

Youth Hostel in Sierra Nevada
Calle Peñones, 22
Tel. 958 48 03 05

EATING AND DRINKING
GOURMET RESTAURANTS
Carmen de San Miguel
A restaurant of "young
Andalusian cuisine" with a
lot going for it, on the slopes
overlooking the Realejo, with
splendid views.
Plaza de Torres Bermejas, 3
Tel. 958 22 67 23

El Claustro
Tradition and creativity are
the key aspects that liven up
the menu of this elegant spot,
enveloped by the historic
atmosphere of the AC

Palacio de Santa Paula hotel,
to which it belongs.
Plaza de Torres Bermejas, 3
Tel. 958 22 67 23

Ruta del Veleta
On the outskirts of Granada,
on the way to Sierra Nevada.
Its offer of creative and
imaginative cuisine, along
with its atmosphere and
service, have rewarded it
with deserved recognition.
An essential reference point
in Granada's gastronomy.
Carretera de Sierra Nevada,
136. Cenes de la Vega.
Tel. 958 48 61 34

**CLASSIC GRANADA
RESTAURANTS**
Chikito
One of the locals' favourite
restaurants, with a recipe
book that represents the
local culinary traditions.
Very central.
Plaza del Campillo, 9
Tel. 958 22 33 64

Mirador de Morayma
In a fantastic walled house in
the heart of the Albaicin within view of the Alhambra, it
has recovered many traditional dishes and recipes with a
certain Al-Andalus echo.
Calle Pianista García Carrillo,
2. Tel. 958 22 82 90

Sevilla
Open in 1930 and frequented
by a renowned clientele, it is
a classic of local gastronomy.
Located opposite the Royal
Chapel. Calle Oficios, 12
Tel. 958 22 12 23

RESTAURANTS
Cunini
Renowned for its fish and
seafood specialities. Also
excellent for tapas and snacks.
Plaza de la Pescadería, 14.
Tel. 958 25 07 77

La Mimbre
Typical Andalusian gastronomy in the seductive setting of
the Alhambra. Next to the

Bar "La Ermita".

entrance to the Generalife.
Tel. 958 22 22 76

La Pesquería
Specialities in seafood, fish
and rice dishes. In the centre,
by the Plaza de la Romanilla.
Calle Capuchinas, 14
Tel. 958 52 15 55

Las Tinajas
Devoted to Granada and
Andalusian cuisine, based on
the very best produce.
Martínez Campos, 17
Tel. 958 25 43 93

Mesón la Pataleta
With a rustic and traditional
atmosphere, specialising in
meat dishes.
Plaza del Gran Capitán, 1.
Tel. 958 28 12 96

Mirador de Aixa
A walled house in the Albaicin
for enjoying the fresh air.
Carril de San Agustín, 2
Tel. 958 22 36 16

Rincón de Miguel
Beside the Avenida de la
Constitución, it has won fame
by its own merits for the creativity of its specialities and
the variety and dynamism of
its menu the whole year
round.
Avenida de los Andaluces, 2
Tel. 958 29 29 78

Parador de San Francisco
Facing the Generalife, with a
marvellous terrace.
Calle Real de la Alhambra,
s/n. Tel. 958 22 14 40

Ceramics.

TAPAS

In Granada the tapa is the inseparable companion of the drink by the bar being served with it automatically and at will by the waiters, who in successive rounds will take the trouble to vary them even though you can order your favourites or order extra tapas and a la carte portions. The places where you can try tapas are spread around the whole city, as would be expected, although they are particularly abundant, along with the lively atmosphere and milling public, in some areas such as the Plaza de San Miguel Bajo and the Plaza Larga in the district of the Albaicin, the Plaza Nueva and the beginning of Calle Elvira, Paseo de los Tristes alongside the Darro, in the area adjoining the Plaza del Carmen and

The Alcaicería.

Puerta Real, and, above all, in the Campo del Príncipe, in the Realejo, with a large concentration of highly popular bars, bodegas and inns.

Bodegas Castañeda
Traditional and very popular meeting point, with the atmosphere of an old-fashioned tavern, next to the Plaza Nueva.
Calle Almireceros, 1 and Elvira, 5
Tel. 958 22 97 06

Braserito
One of the most reputed in Campo del Príncipe, with a very busy terrace.
Campo del Príncipe, s/n
Tel. 958 22 19 84

Casa Enrique
One of the most old-fashioned tapas bars in Granada, close to Puerta Real.
Acera del Darro, 8
Tel 958 25 50 08

La Esquinita
Variety and originality reign in this spot with a wide-ranging repertoire.
Campo del Príncipe, s/n
Tel. 958 22 71 06

El huerto de Juan Ranas
Next to the San Nicolás viewpoint, at the top of the Albaicin.
Calle Atarazana Vieja, 6
Tel. 958 28 69 25

Gran Taberna
With an old-fashioned atmosphere. Very central.

Plaza Nueva, 12
Tel. 958 22 88 46

Tendido 1
Spacious spot in the lower part of the bullring.
Cold meats, cheeses, meats.
Avenida Doctor Olóriz, 25
Tel. 954 41 68 11

GRANADA AT NIGHT

The very setting, the climate and the high student population all contribute to a lively nightlife in Granada. Among the historic areas with most atmosphere feature the Campo del Príncipe and the Albaicin, and even later into the night, Plaza Nueva and the beginning of Calle Elvira, Carrera del Darro and Paseo de los Tristes, and some corners of the Albaicin. In the more modern parts, a lot of people are Attracted to the area around Calle Pedro Antonio de Alarcón and the surrounding area and other parts, such as Plaza de Gracia.

FLAMENCO

The roots of flamenco in Granada, which has provided an unending list of first-class artists, is shown in the dances and shows by gypsy groups from the caves of the Sacromonte, along with those that take place in the concert halls of other traditional districts.

Los Canasteros
Carril de San Cecilio, s/n
El Realejo.
Tel. 958 22 11 00

Los Tarantos
Camino del Sacromonte, 9
Tel. 958 22 45 25

Sala Albaicin
Carretera de Murcia, mirador de San Cristóbal.
Tel. 958 80 46 46

Venta El Gallo
Barranco de los Negros, 5
Sacromonte. Tel. 958 22 05 91

**Zambra de María la
Canastera**
Sacromonte, 89
Tel. 958 12 11 93

SHOPPING
SHOPPING AREAS

Puerta Real, Calle Ángel
Ganivet, Reyes Católicos, Gran
Vía de Colón and their
surrounding areas are the centre of the modern shopping
area, adjoining the traditional
areas of Calle Mesones, Plaza
Bib Rambla or the Realejo. The
Zacatín, and the Alcaicería
precinct, and Calle Elvira are
also centres with a high level
of activity, with a well-known
presence of handicrafts, which
also dominate in the Cuesta
de Gomérez and the Albaicín.
There are also shops in the
more modern areas and in the
big commercial centres close
to the Camino de Ronda and
the bypass.
SHOPS
Antigüedades Aladino
In the street of the antique
dealers par excellence.
Calle Elvira, 40
Artesanía Morillo
Ceramics, marquetry
Cuesta de Gomérez, 37
Tel. 958 22 58 84
Bazar Oriental
Marquetry, leather goods,
costume jewellery.
Calle Paños, 6
Tel. 958 22 80 45
Casa Ferrer
Guitars.
Cuesta de Gomérez, 26
Tel. 954 22 84 95
Casa Ysla
The inventors of the most
authentic Granada sweet, the
pionono, and other pastry
delights.
Acera del Darro, 62, Carrera
del Genil, 27 and Avenida de
la Constitución, 48
Tel. 958 52 30 88

Cerámica de Fajalauza
Granada ceramics and pot-
tery. Carretera de Murcia
(Albaicín) and Plaza de San
Isidro, 5
Estévez
The typical Granada
lampposts in tin and glass.
Calle Alhóndiga, 39
Francisco Mariscal
Granada handicrafts.
Calle Alcaicería, 11
Tel. 958 22 30 11
**Guitarrería Bellido y
Gil de Avalle**
String instruments.
Plaza del Realejo, 15
Tel. 958 22 16 10
López Mezquita
Traditional pastries in an old-
fashioned spot right in the
centre.
Calle Reyes Católicos, 29
Mantequerías Castellano
Local gastronomy specialities.
Calle Almireceros, 6
Tel. 958 22 48 40
Mima
Great variety of embroidered
shawls, lace mantilla, fans
and complements.
Calle Reyes Católicos, 18
Tel. 958 22 32 91
SPANISH LABELS
In the centre, from Puerta
Real to the Gran Vía, there
are many shops of Spanish
labels such as Loewe,

Roberto Verino, Benetton,
Cortefiel, El Caballo or Adolfo
Domínguez, among others.
STREET MARKETS
In some streets and squares
the shops are grouped together
forming veritable bazaars.
Thus, in Cuesta de Gomérez,
Alcaicería and the streets of
the Albaicín Alto are full of
shops selling local crafts,
while Calderería Vieja and
Nueva are staked out with
shops selling Moroccan goods
and tea houses. Plaza Larga in
the Albaicín and the Plaza del
Realejo have a definite character of a street market, while in
the Plaza Bib Rambla there are
many flower stalls, and around
the cathedral, spice stalls.

FAIRS AND
CONGRESSES
**Exhibition and Congress
Hall of Granada**
Paseo del Violón, s/n
Tel. 958 24 67 00
A building of contemporary
design alongside the River
Genil with more than 45,000
m2 on seven levels. It contains
rooms, auditoriums, exhibition
areas and other spaces in
which a varied programme of
fairs and meetings is organised throughout the year.
www.pcgr.org

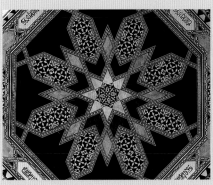

Marquetry.

Index

A

Abbey of the Sacromonte, 44
Abencerrajes Hall, 24
Albaicin, 6, 8, 14, 20, 35-45
Albaicin Alto, 40, 41
Albaicin Bajo, 37
Alcaicería, 50
Alcazaba, 6, 16, 19
Alcazaba Cadima (o Vieja), 42
Alcázar Genil, 74
Alhama de Granada, 84
Alhambra, 8, 9, 13-33, 40, 42
Alhambra Alta (o el Secano),
28, 29
Almijara, 84
Almuñécar, 81, 82
Ambassadors Hall, 22
Arch de las Pesas, 42
Archaeological Museum (or
Casa de Castril), 38
Arms Tower, 19
Arrayanes Courtyard (or the
Alberca courtyard), 22

B

Barca Room, 22
Basílica of Nuestra Señora
de las Angustias, 73
Baths of Polinario, 29
Baza, 85
Bermejas Towers, 16
Botanical Garden, 62
Bubión, 80
Busquístar, 80

C

Cadí Bridge, 38
Cádiar, 81
Calle Ángel Ganivet, 48

Calle Calderería, 44
Calle Elvira, 36
Calle del Agua, 41
Calle del Zacatín, 50
Calle Oficios, 52
Calle Real, 28
Campo del Príncipe, 71
Capileira, 80
Carmen de los Mártires, 71
Carrera del Darro, 36, 37
Carrera del Genil, 73
Casa de Castril (see
Archaeological Museum)
Casa de los Mascarones, 41
Casa de los Pisa, 37
Casa de los Tiros, 70
Casas del Chapiz (School of
Arab Studies), 41
Castell de Ferro, 82
Cathedral, 9, 56-58
Cathedral Museum, 56
Church of San Miguel Bajo, 43
Church of San Pedro y San
Pablo, 40
Church of Santa Ana, 37
Church of Santa María de la
Alhambra, 29
Church of Santo Domingo, 72
Church of the Sagrario, 58
Church of the Salvador, 41
Church of the Santos Justo
y Pastor, 62
Collegiate of de San Cecilio,
44
Comares (palace, façade,
tower), 20, 22
Convent of San Francisco
(Parador Hotel), 29
Convent of Santa Catalina
de Zafra, 38
Córdoba Palace, 41
Corral del Carbón, 49

Courtyard of Polo, 32
Courtyard of the Acequia, 32
Courtyard of the Sultana, 32
Cuesta de la Alhacaba, 41
Cuesta del Chapiz, 40

D

District of Mauror, 72
District of the Almanzora, 37

E

Ecclesiastical Curia, 58
Emperor's Rooms, 24
Exhibition and Congress
Hall, 74

F

Fuente Vaqueros, 83
Fundación Rodríguez
Acosta, 72

G

Garden of the Adarves, 19
Gateway of Justice, 18
Gateway of the
Pomegranates, 16
Gateway of the Seven
Floors, 30
Gateway of Wine, 18, 28
Gomérez Hill, 16
Gran Vía de Colón, 10, 48
Guadix, 84, 85

H

Hall of the Two Sisters, 24
Hermitage of San Sebastián,
74

Hermitage of Santo Sepulcro, 44
High Gardens, 32
Holy Caves, 44
Hospital and church of San Juan de Dios, 64
Hospital Real (Royal Hospital), 9, 65, 66
House-Museum of Manuel de Falla, 72
Huerta de San Vicente, 74, 75

J

Juviles, 80

K

King's Hall, 24

L

La Calahorra, 85
La Herradura, 82
Lanjarón, 80
Laroles, 81
Lindaraja Viewpoint, 24
Loja, 83
Lonja de Mercaderes, 54

M

Machuca Courtyard, 20
Madraza, 52
Marquesado del Zenete, 85
Max Moreau Museum, 43
Mecina Bombarón, 80
Mexuar (Hall, Oratory, Golden Room), 20
Moclín, 83
Monastery of San Jerónimo, 9, 62, 63
Monastery of Santa Isabel la Real, 43
Montefrío, 83
Museum of Fine Arts, 28

N

Natural Park of the Alhama, Tejeda and Almijara, 84
Natural Park of the Sierra de Huétor, 84
New or Low Gardens, 30

O

Órgiva, 80

P

Palace of Charles V, 28
Palace of Dar Al-Horra, 42
Palace of the Generalife, 32
Palace of the Lions, 23
Palace of Yusuf III, 26
Pampaneira, 80
Parade Ground, 19
Parroquia de San Matías, 70
Paseo de la Bomba, 74
Paseo de los Cipreses, 30
Paseo de los Tristes, 40
Paseo del Salón, 74
Paseo del Violón, 74
Picos Tower, 26
Pillar of Charles V, 18
Pitres, 80
Plaza Bib Rambla, 50
Plaza de Isabel la Católica, 48
Plaza de Mariana Pineda, 73
Plaza del Carmen, 49
Plaza de la Pescadería, 58
Plaza de la Romanilla, 58
Plaza de la Trinidad, 62
Plaza de la Universidad, 62
Plaza de las Pasiegas, 58
Plaza de los Aljibes, 18
Plaza Larga, 41, 42
Plaza Nueva, 36
Pórtugos, 80
Puerta de Elvira, 65
Puerta Real, 48
Puerto de la Ragua, 85

Q

Queen's Dressing Room, 24

R

Royal Chancery, 9, 37
Royal Chapel, 9, 29, 52-55
Royal Hall of Santo Domingo, 72

S

Salobreña, 81

San Cecilio alleyway, 42
Santa Fe, 9, 82
Science Park, 74, 75
Sentry Tower, 19
Sierra Nevada, 78, 79
Sierra Nevada National Park, 78

T

The Alpujarra, 79-81
The Antequeruela, 71
The Bañuelo, 38
The Cartuja, 65, 66
The Costa Tropical, 81, 82
The Generalife, 30
The Partal, 24
The Realejo, 70
The Royal Baths, 24
The Sacromonte, 44
Tejeda, 84
Torrenueva, 82
Tower of the Cautiva, 26
Tower of the Infantas, 26
Town Hall, 49
Trevélez, 80
Triunfo Gardens, 64

U

Ugíjar, 81

V

Válor, 80
Viewpoint of La Lona, 43
Viewpoint of San Nicolás, 42

W

Water Stairway, 32

Y

Yegen, 80

Z

Zirid walls, 41

We would like to thank all the organisations and people who, through their cooperation, have made it possible to publish this book.

Published by: Ediciones Aldeasa
Editorial coordination: Carmen de Francisco

Text: Fernando Olmedo
Translation: Steve Cedar
Photography: Archivo Ediciones Aldeasa
All the photos in this guide have been taken by Hidalgo-Lopesino except for those which are detailed below:
Archivo Ediciones Aldeasa, 21b, 27b, 45, 49b, 51a, 52b, 53a, 53b, 55a, 55b, 56, 57a, 57b, 73c, 75a.
Iberimage, 63b, 67a.

Graphic design: Estudio OdZ
Layout: Mariana Grekoff
Cartography: Pedro Monzo
Photomechanics: Cromotex
Printed by: Brizzolis